CONTENTS

AS LONG AS YOU'RE MINE

Music and Lyrics by
STEPHEN SCHWARTZ

With quiet passion

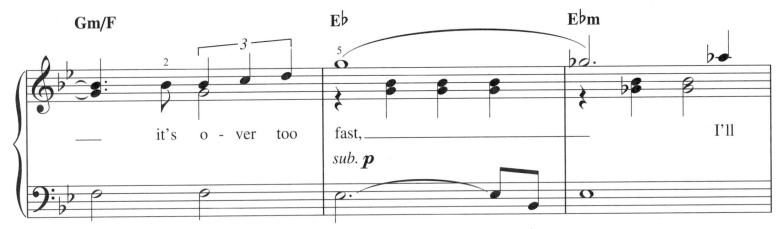

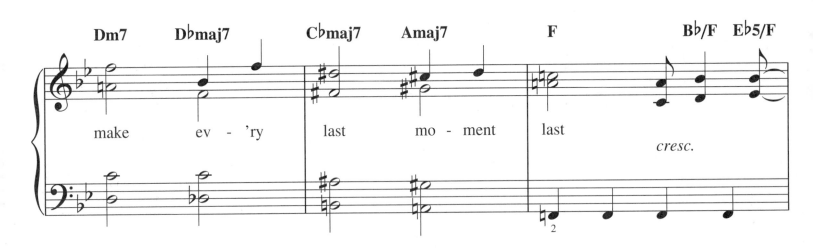

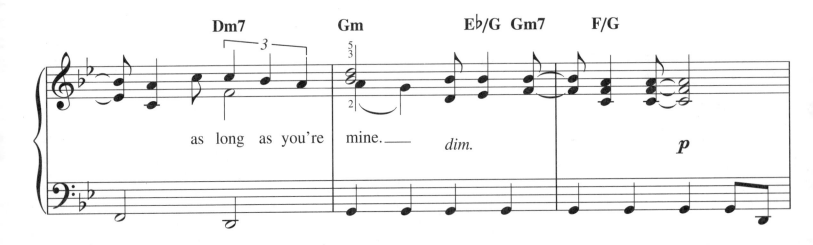

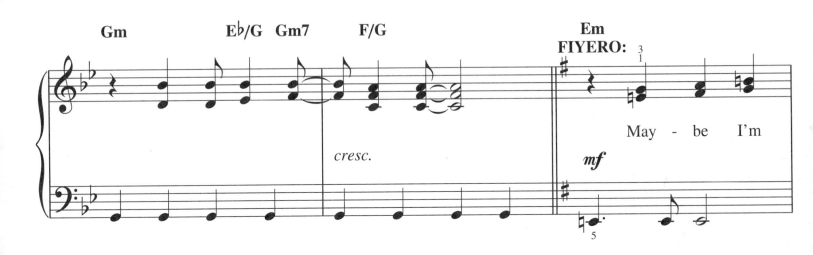

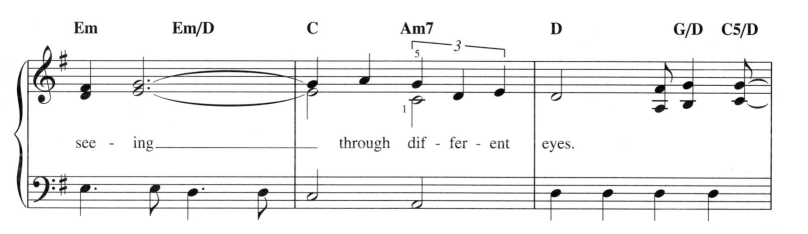

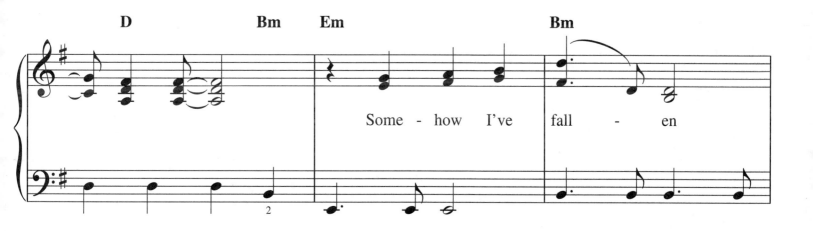

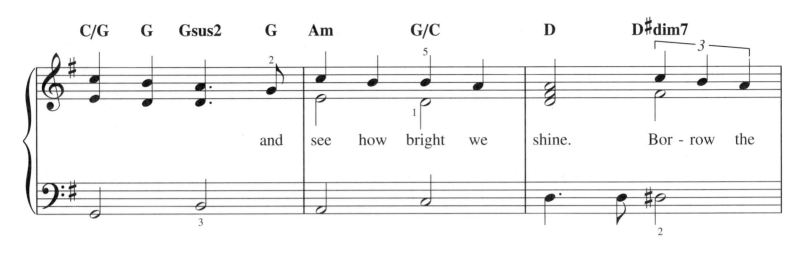

and see how bright we shine. Bor - row the

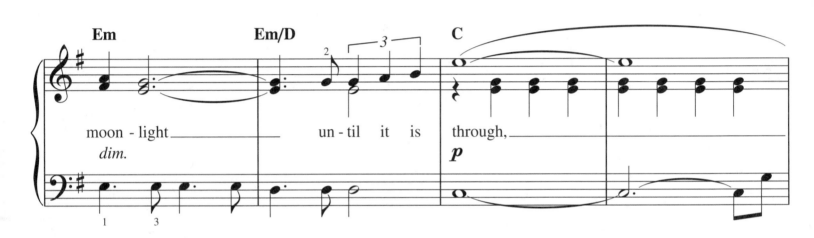

moon - light
dim.
un - til it is through, ___
p

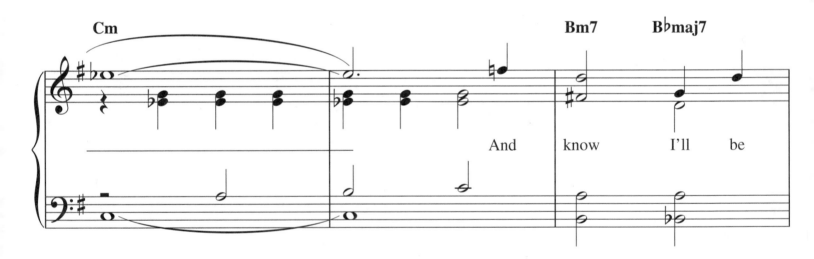

And know I'll be

here hold - ing you

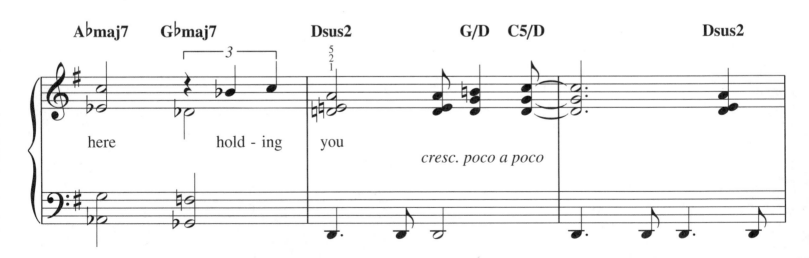

cresc. poco a poco

as long as you're mine...

DANCING THROUGH LIFE

Music and Lyrics by
STEPHEN SCHWARTZ

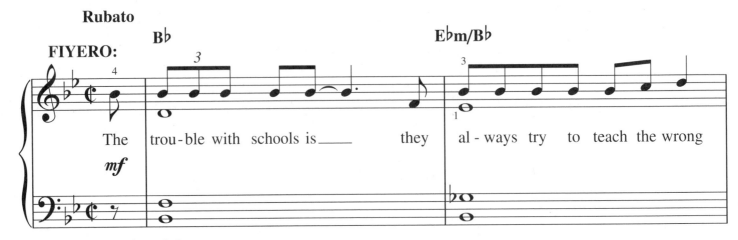

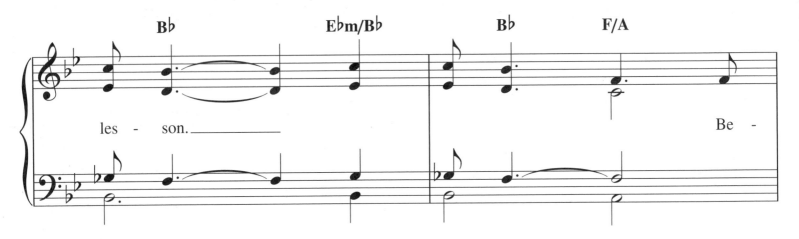

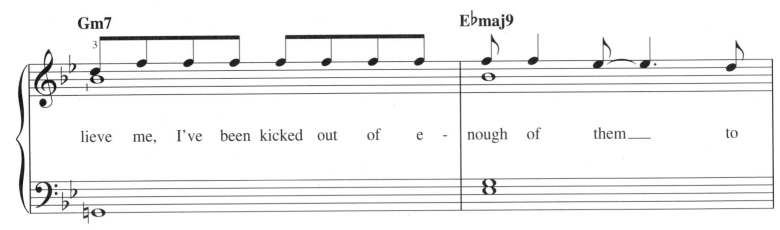

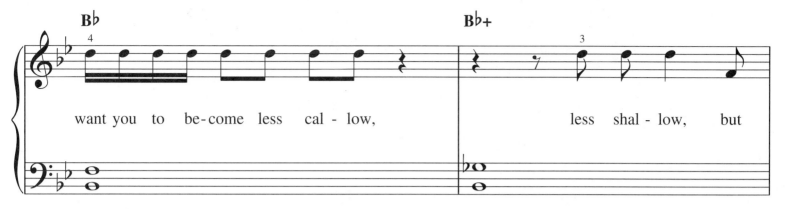

want you to be-come less cal - low,   less shal - low,   but

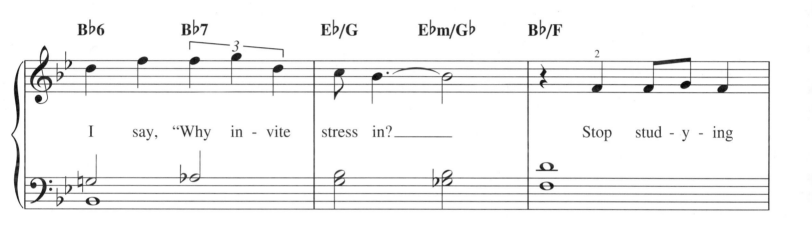

I   say, "Why in - vite   stress in?____   Stop   stud - y - ing

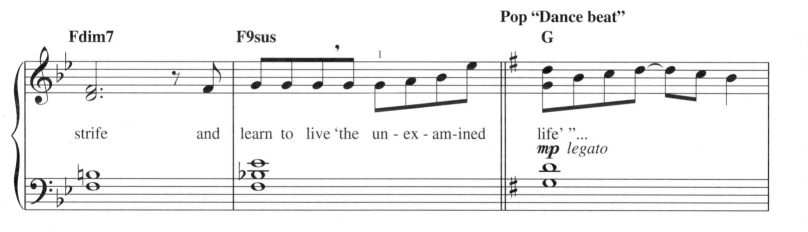

strife   and   learn to live 'the un - ex - am-ined   life' "...
mp legato

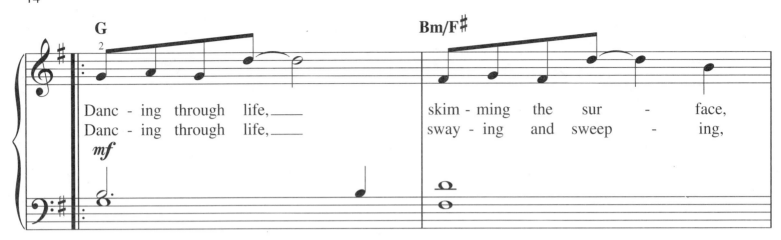

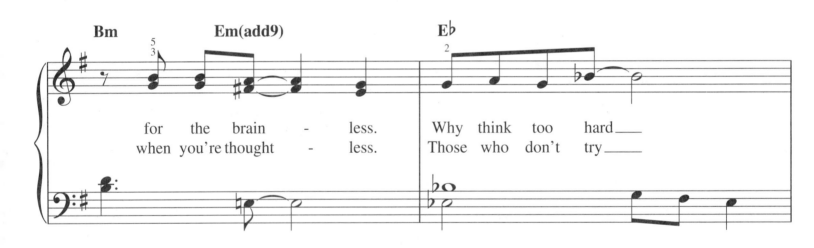

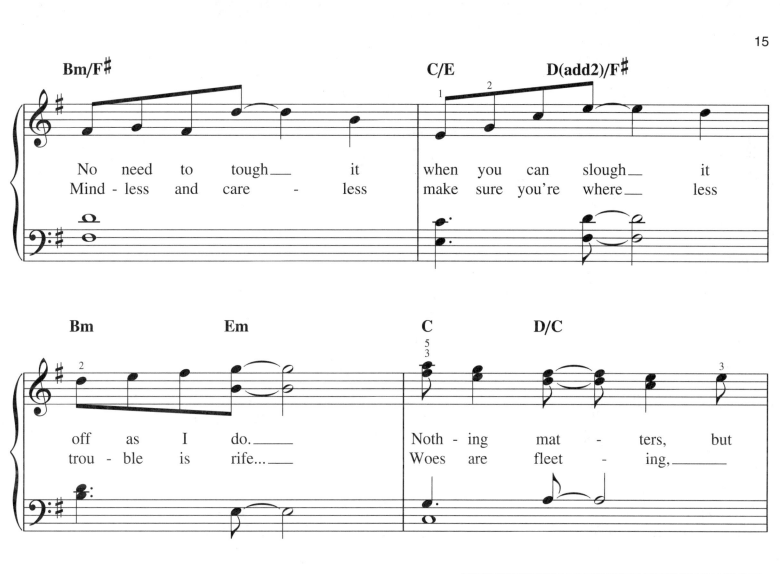

No need to tough___ it when you can slough___ it
Mind - less and care - less make sure you're where___ less

off as I do.___ Noth - ing mat - ters, but
trou - ble is rife...___ Woes are fleet - ing,___

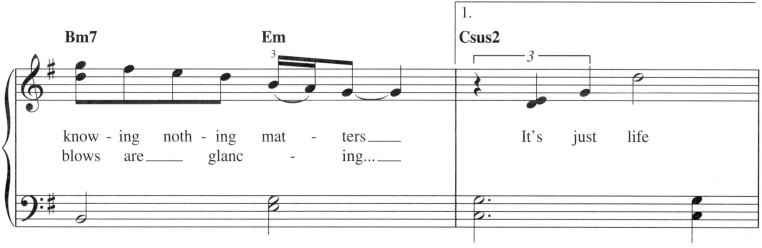

know - ing noth - ing mat - ters___ It's just life
blows are___ glanc - ing...___

1.

so keep danc - ing through...

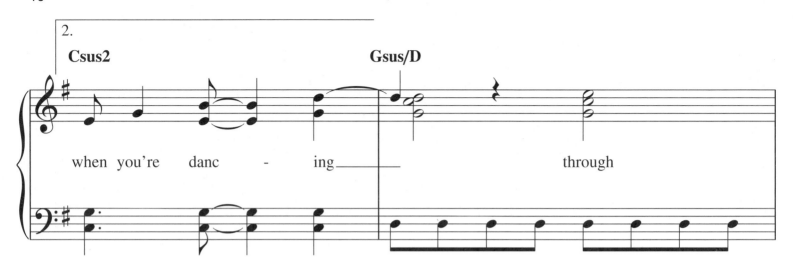

light._____ Find the pret - ti - est girl..._ Give 'er a whirl_____

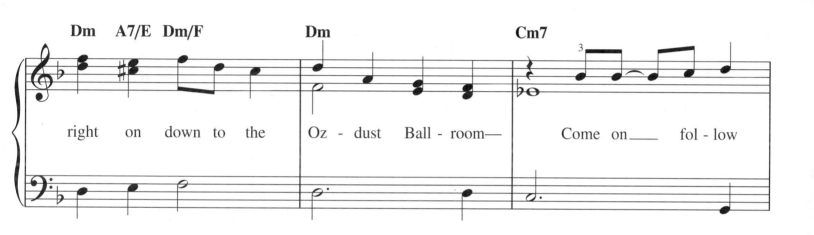

right on down to the Oz - dust Ball - room— Come on___ fol - low

me,___ you'll be hap-py to be there...___

cresc.

Danc - ing through life,___ down at the Oz - dust, if

f

on - ly be - cause_ dust is | what we come to..._ | Noth - ing mat - ters but

know - ing noth - ing mat - ters_ | It's just life *mf* *cresc.* |

f | so keep danc - ing | through.

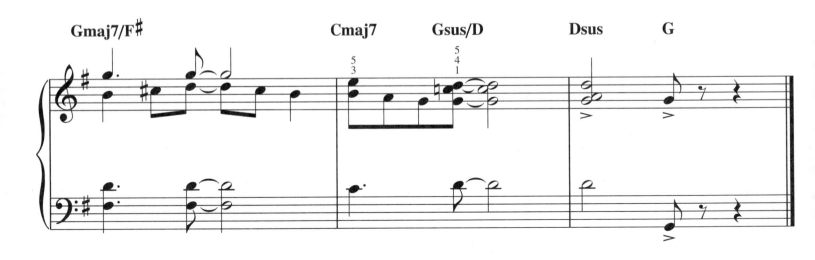

FOR GOOD

Music and Lyrics by
STEPHEN SCHWARTZ

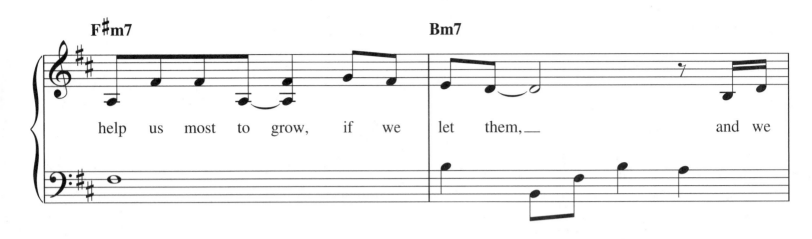

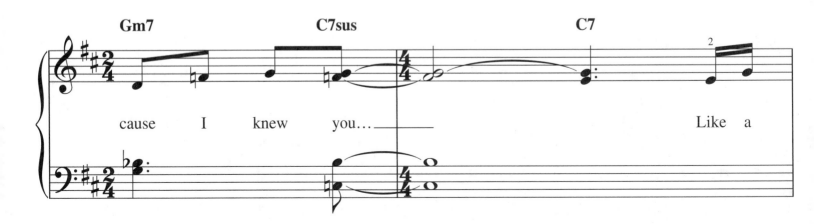

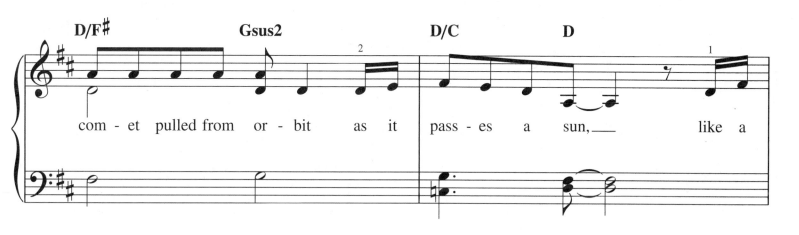

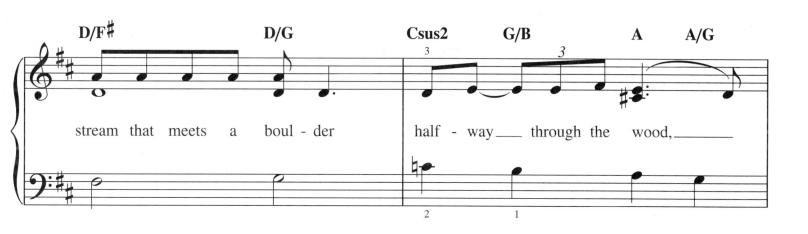

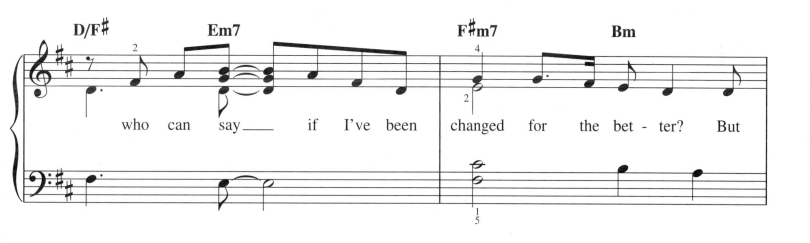

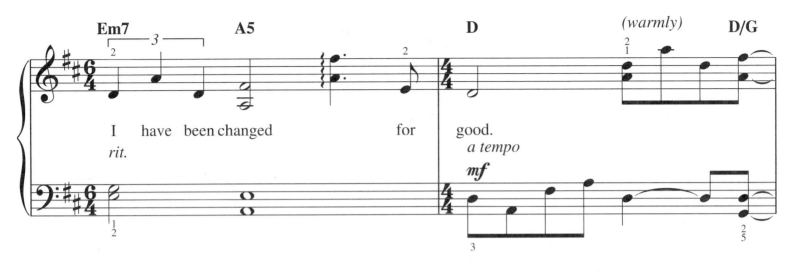

I have been changed for good.

ELPHABA:
It well may be that we will

nev - er meet a - gain in this life - time, so let me

say be - fore we part; So much of me is made of

23

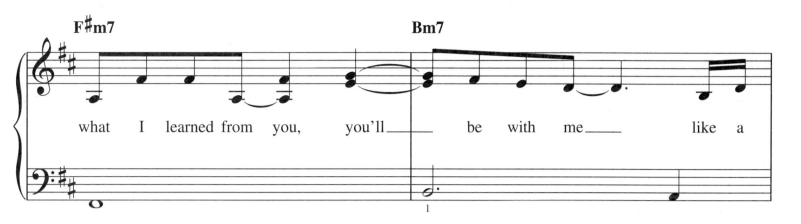

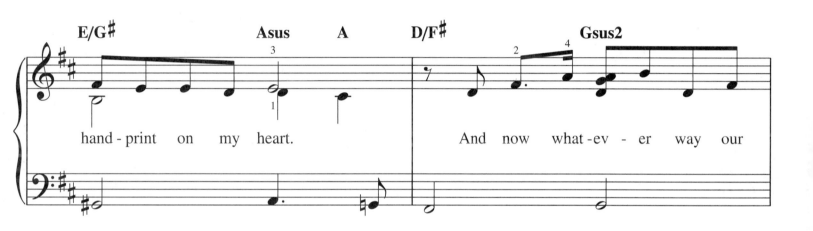

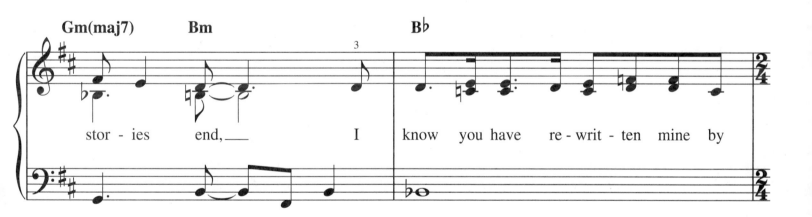

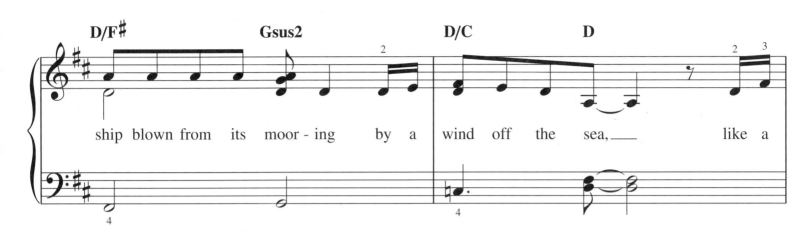

ship blown from its moor - ing by a wind off the sea,___ like a

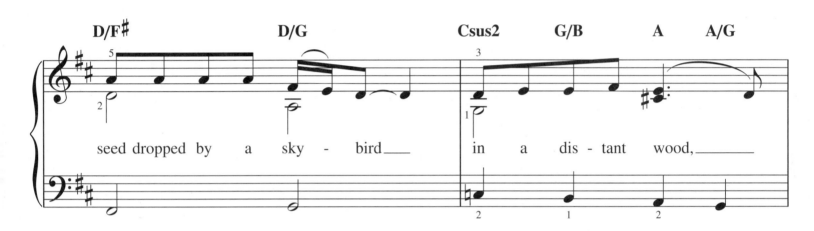

seed dropped by a sky - bird___ in a dis - tant wood,___

who can say___ if I've___ been changed for the bet - ter? But

dim.

be-cause I knew you... Be-cause I knew you... I have been changed for

p   *cresc.*

GLINDA: BOTH:

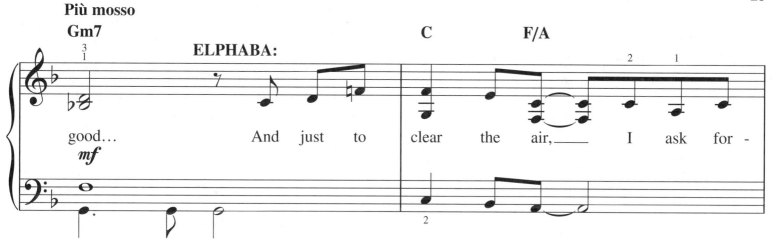

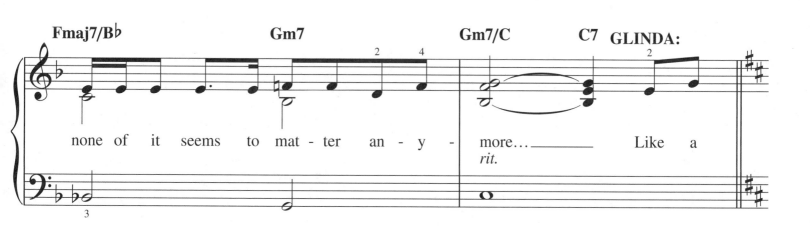

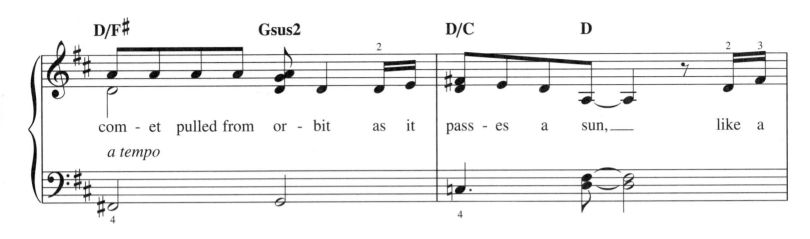

com - et pulled from or - bit as it pass - es a sun,___ like a

a tempo

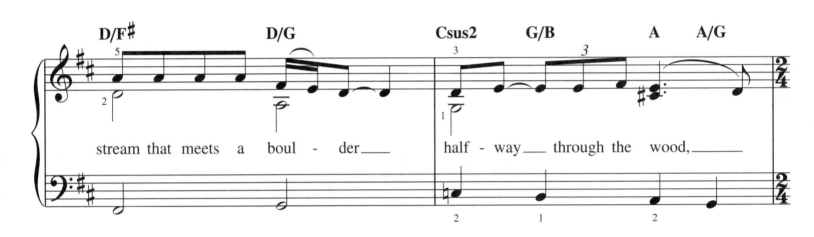

stream that meets a boul - der___ half - way___ through the wood,___

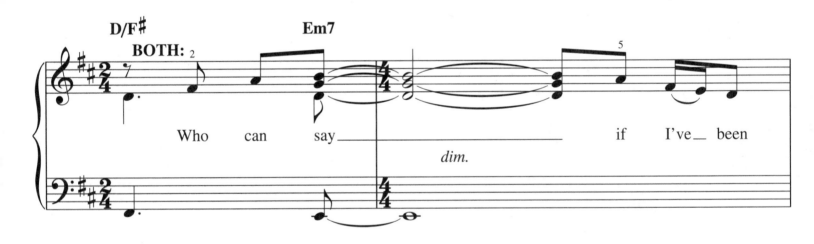

BOTH:

Who can say_____ if I've__ been

dim.

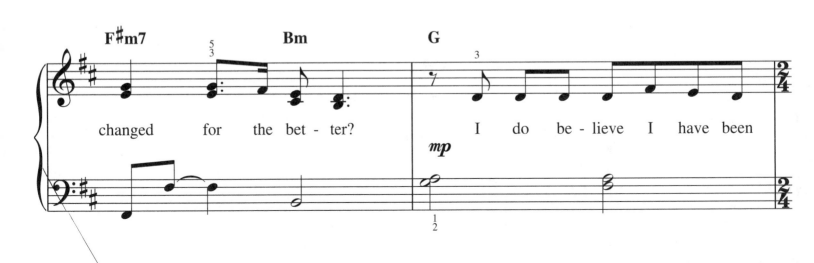

changed for the bet - ter? I do be - lieve I have been

mp

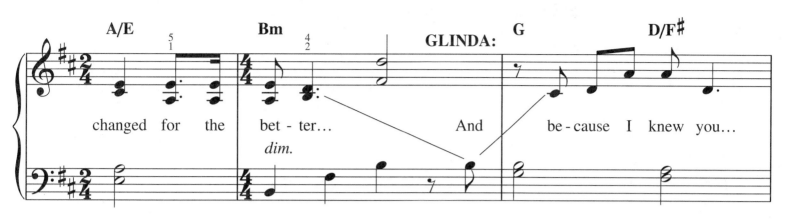

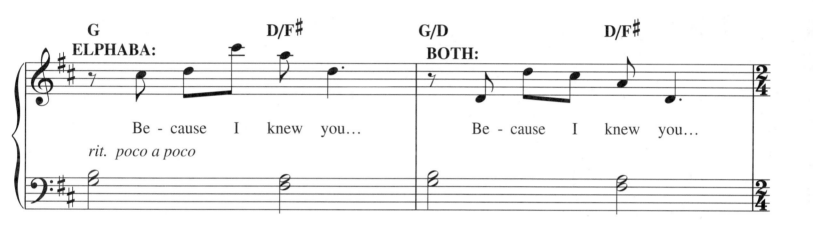

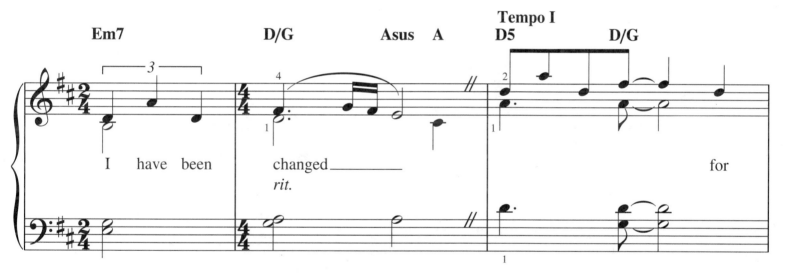

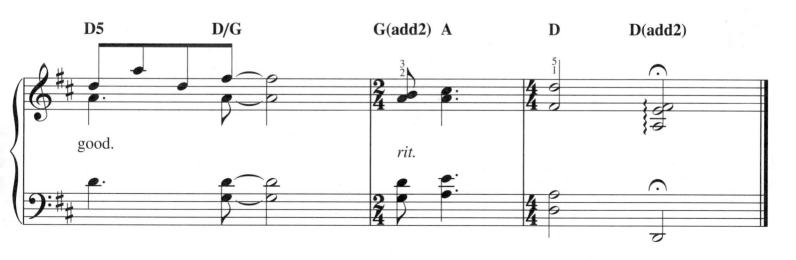

DEFYING GRAVITY

Music and Lyrics by
STEPHEN SCHWARTZ

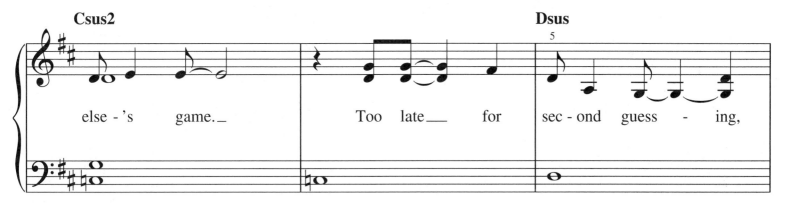

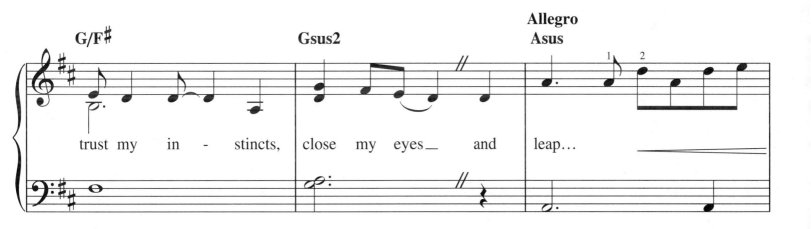

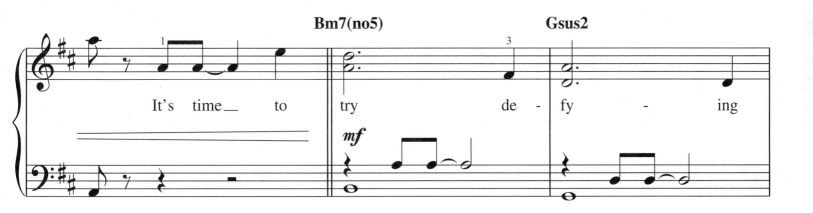

Asus   **Bm7(no5)**

grav - i - ty_____   I think__ I'll   try   de -

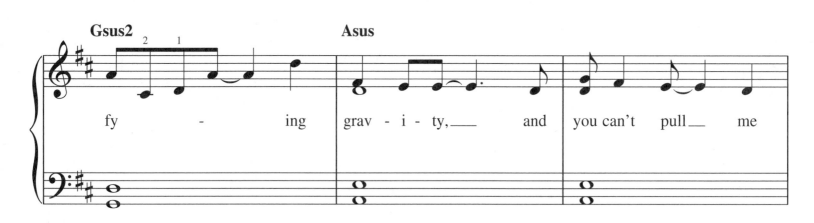

Gsus2   **Asus**

fy -   ing   grav - i - ty,___   and   you can't   pull__ me

D5   **A/E D/F♯ Gsus2**   **D5**   **A/E D/F♯ Gsus2**

down.

                                  D5   **A/E   D/F♯   Gsus2   A(add4)**

                                  I'm through ac - cept - ing   lim -   its

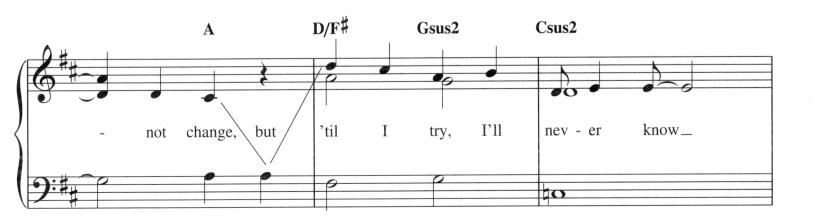

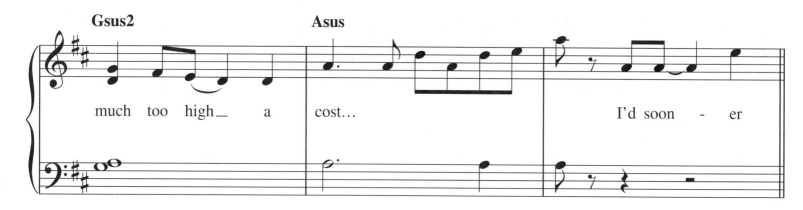

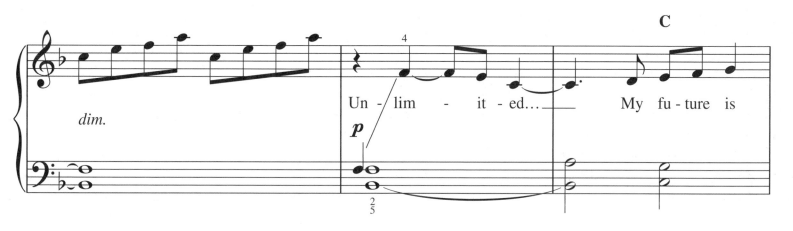

Un - lim - it - ed... My fu - ture is

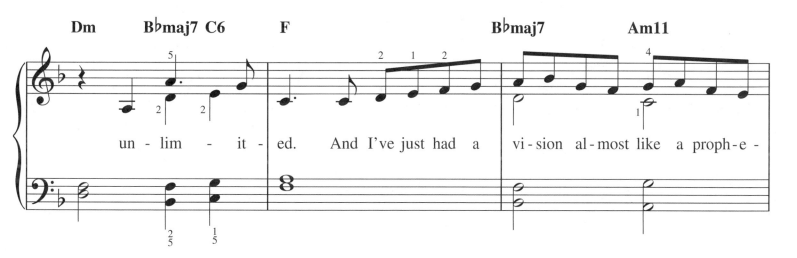

un - lim - it - ed. And I've just had a vi - sion al-most like a proph-e -

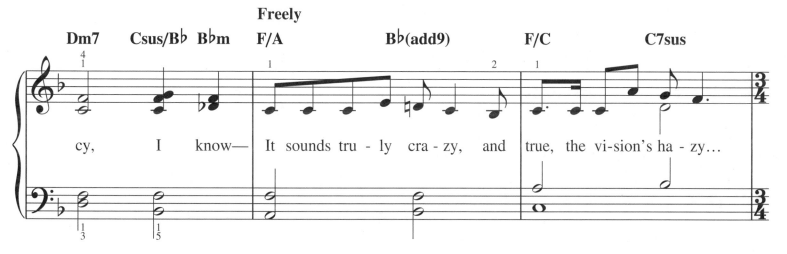

cy, I know— It sounds tru - ly cra - zy, and true, the vi-sion's ha - zy...

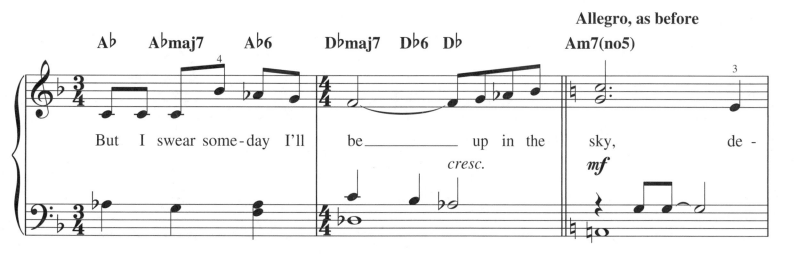

But I swear some-day I'll be_____ up in the sky, de -

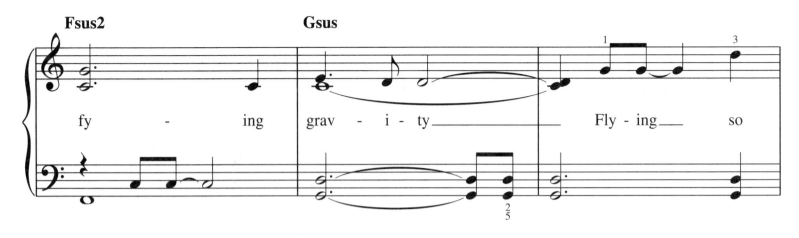

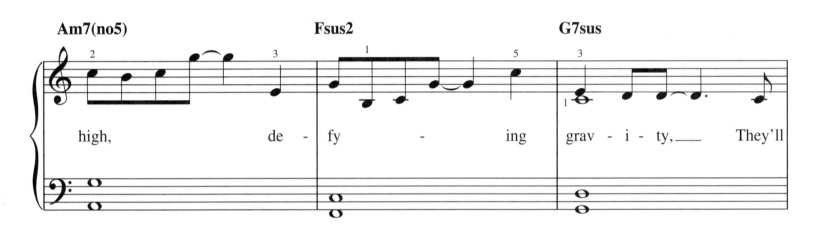

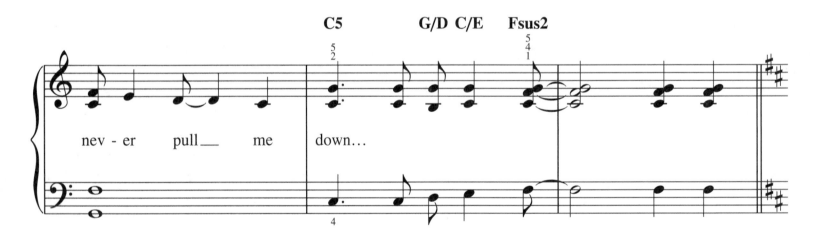

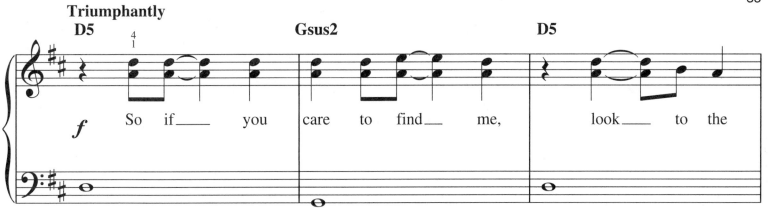

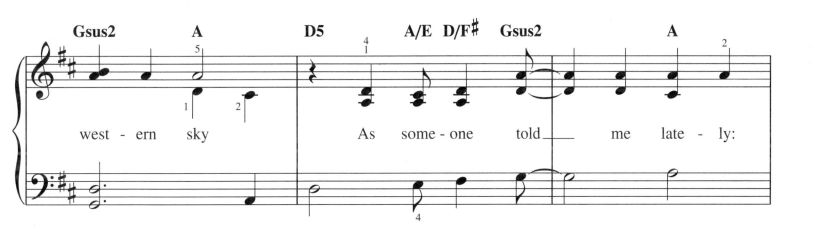

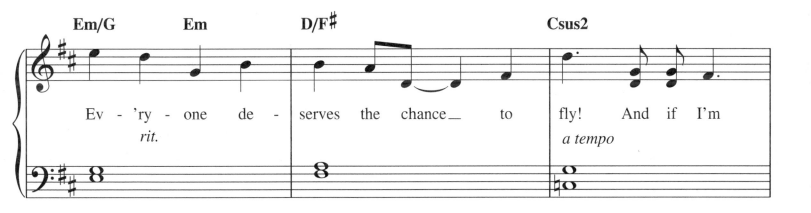

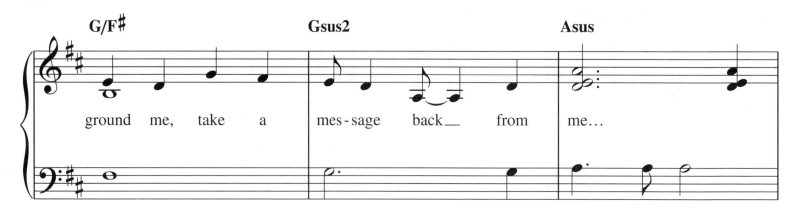

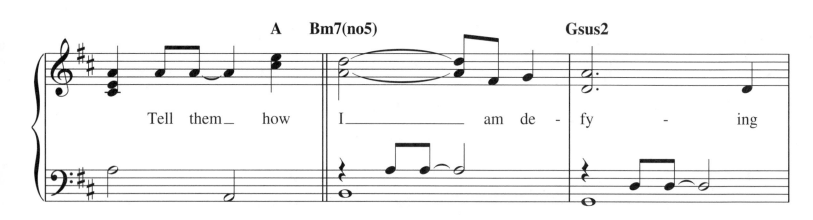

With determination, slower

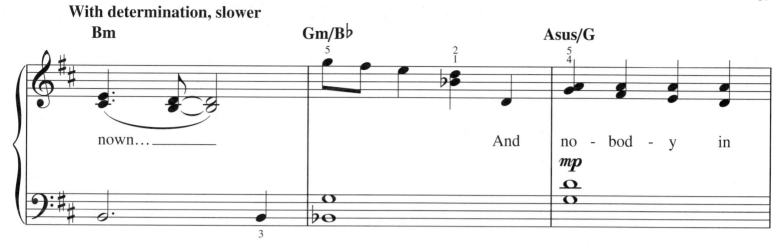

nown… And no - bod - y in

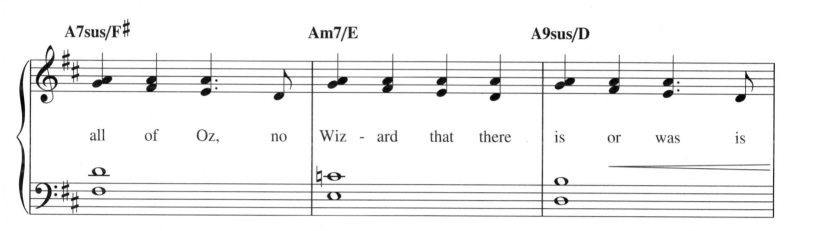

all of Oz, no Wiz - ard that there is or was is

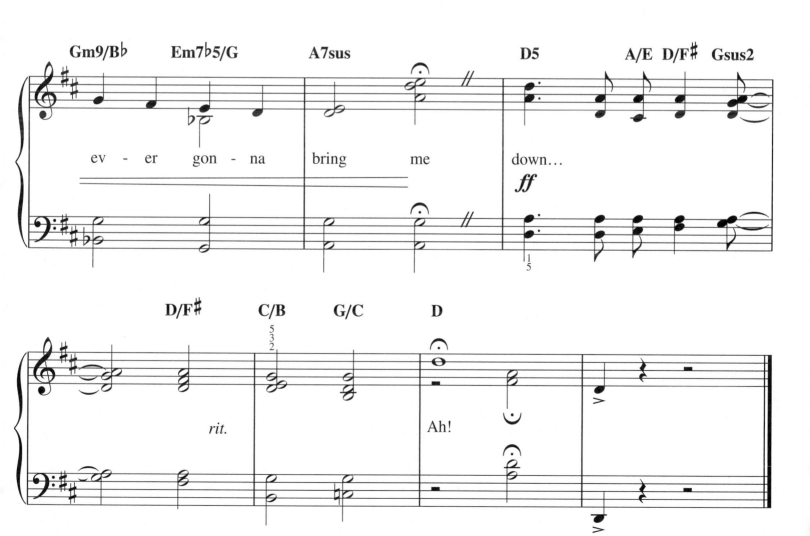

ev - er gon - na bring me down…

down…

rit.

Ah!

I'M NOT THAT GIRL

Music and Lyrics by
STEPHEN SCHWARTZ

Sweet and steady, like a music box

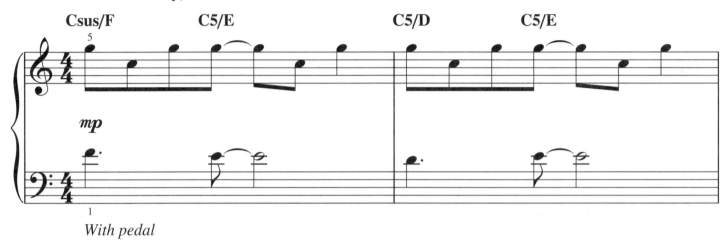

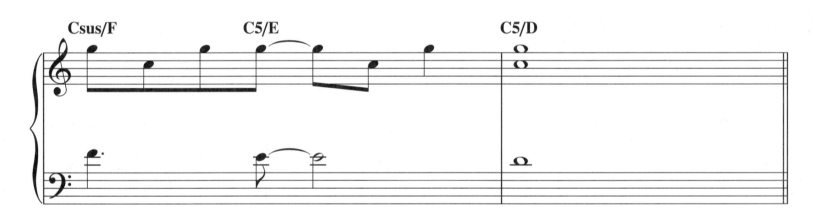

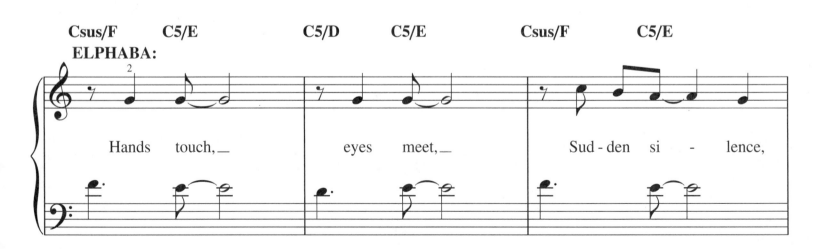

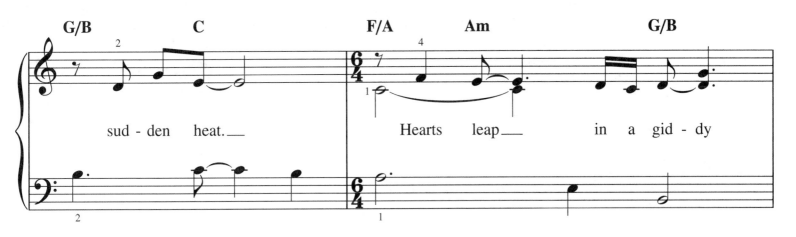

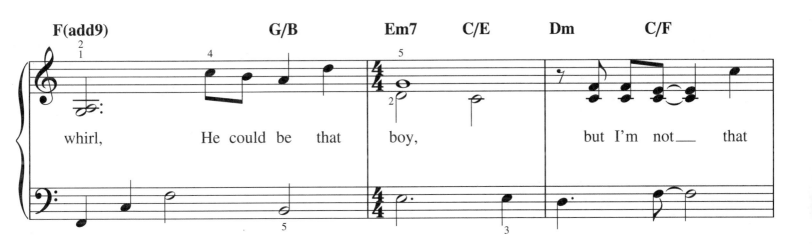

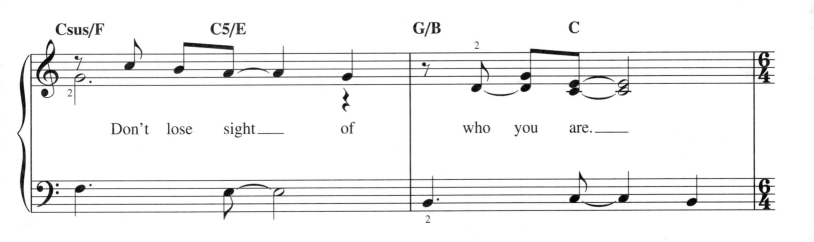

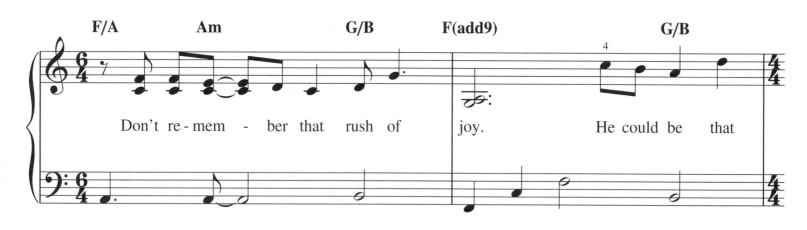

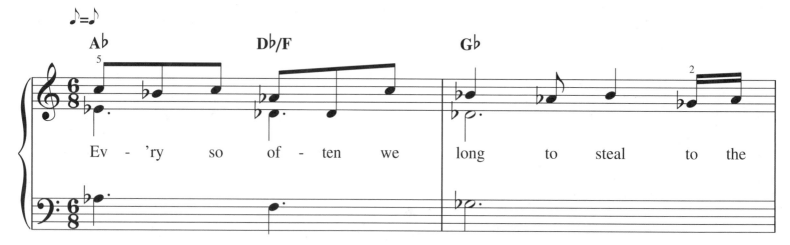

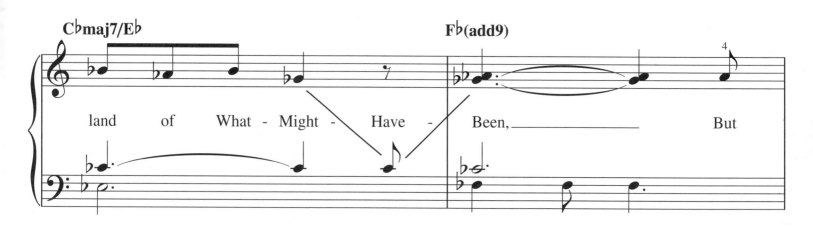

41

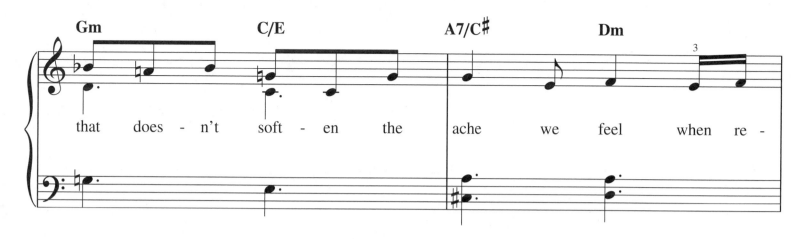

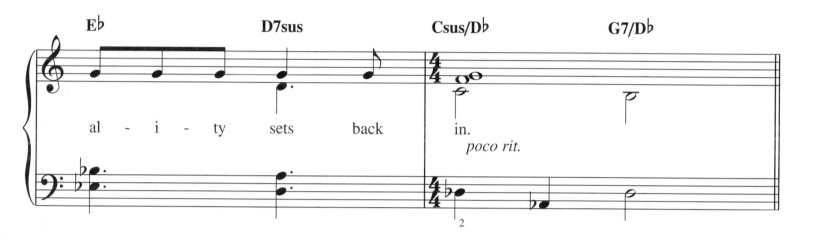

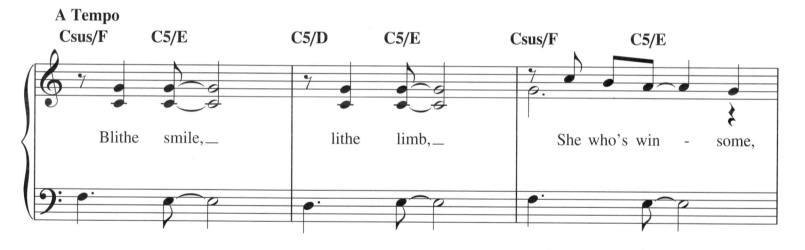

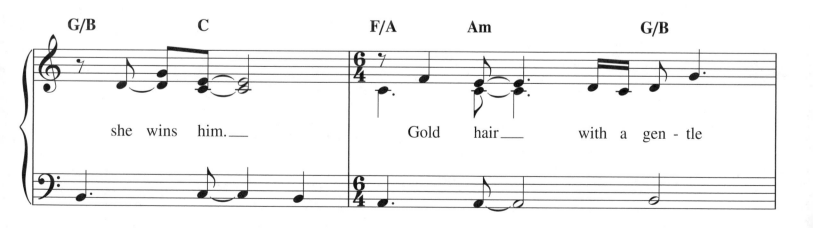

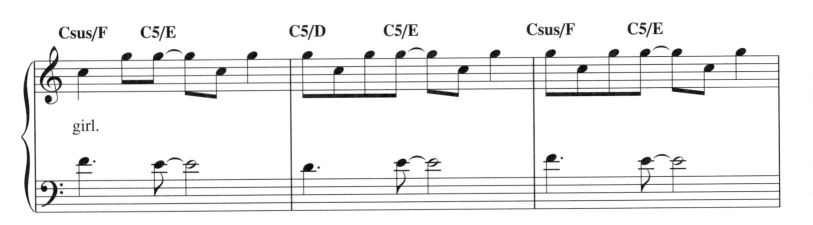

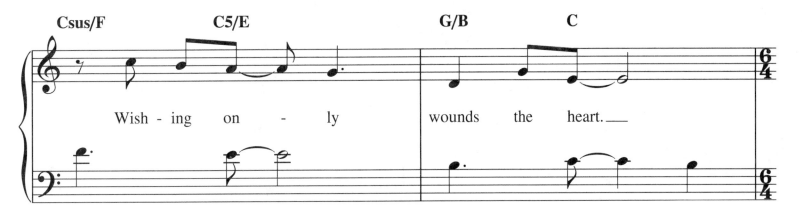

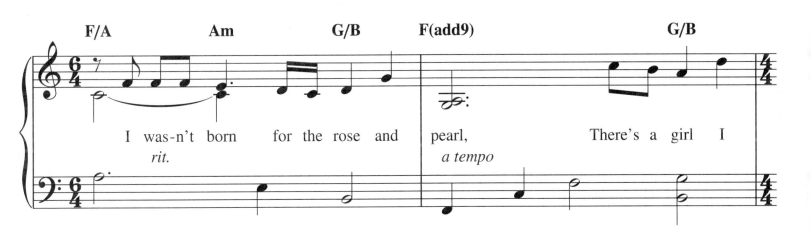

POPULAR

Music and Lyrics by
STEPHEN SCHWARTZ

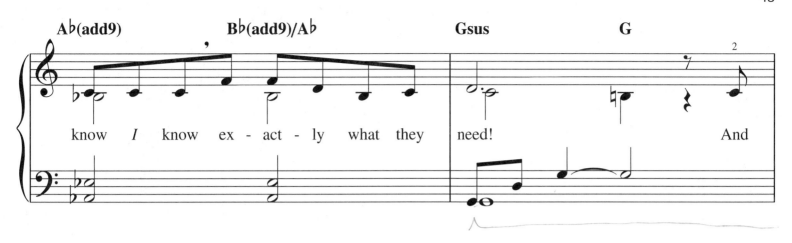

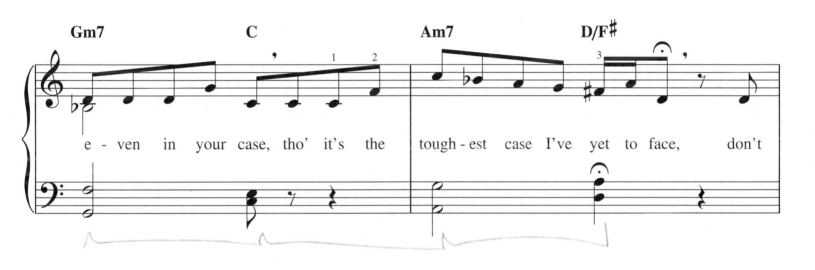

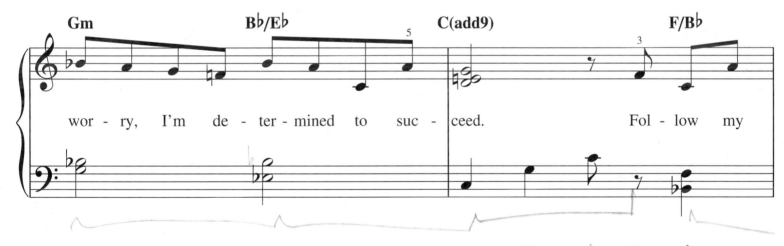

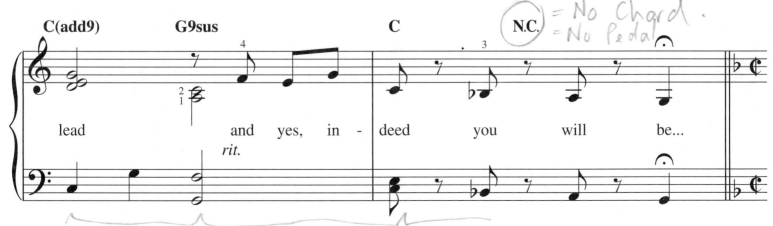

know   So let's start, 'cause you've got an aw-f'lly long way to

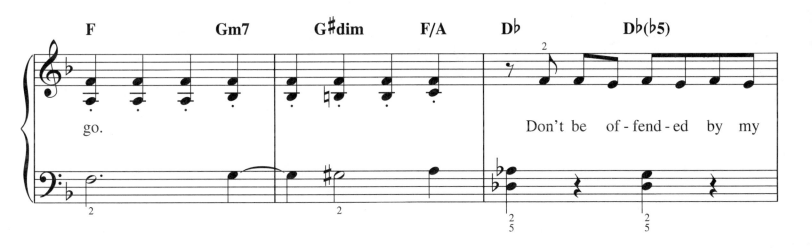

go.   Don't be of-fend-ed by my

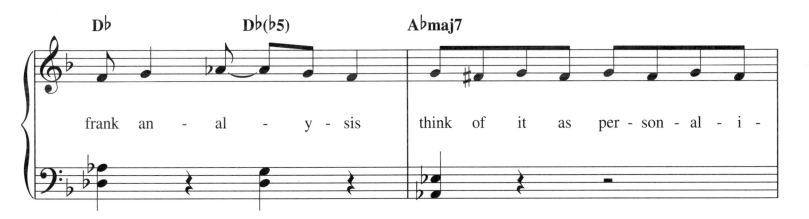

frank an - al - y - sis   think of it as per-son-al-i-

ty di - al - y - sis.   Now that I've chos-en to be-

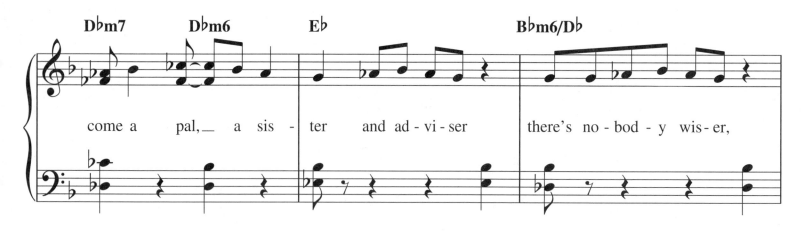

come a pal,__ a sis - ter and ad - vi - ser there's no - bod - y wis - er,

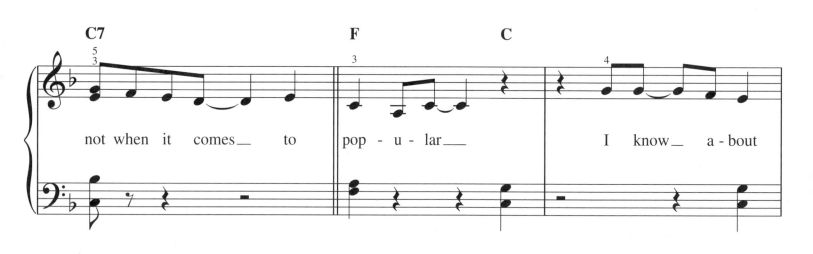

not when it comes__ to pop - u - lar__ I know__ a - bout

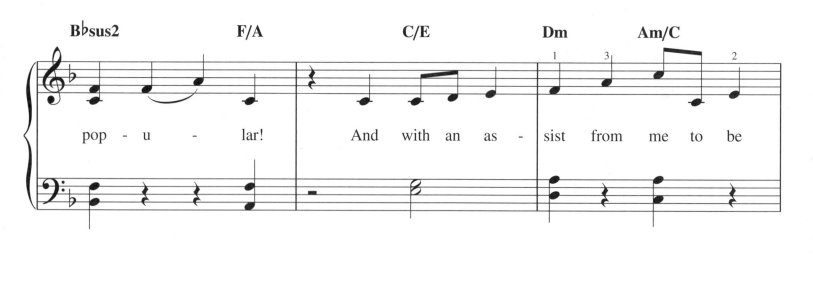

pop - u - lar! And with an as - sist from me to be

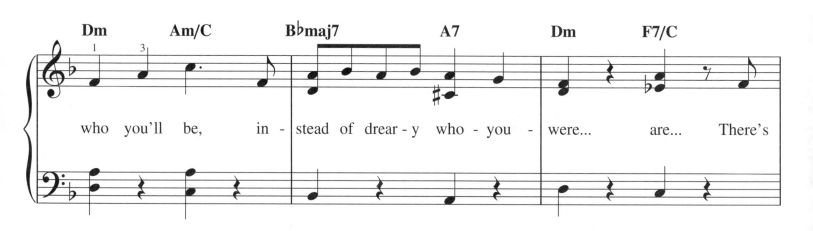

who you'll be, in - stead of drear - y who - you - were... are... There's

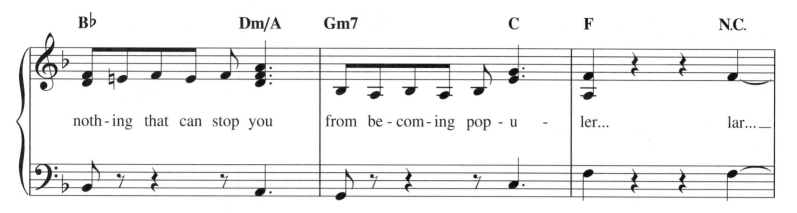

noth-ing that can stop you | from be-com-ing pop-u- ler... lar...

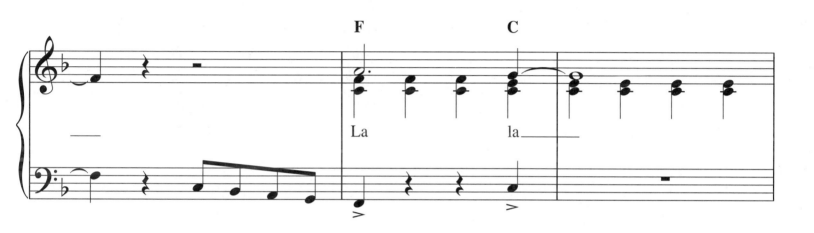

La la la

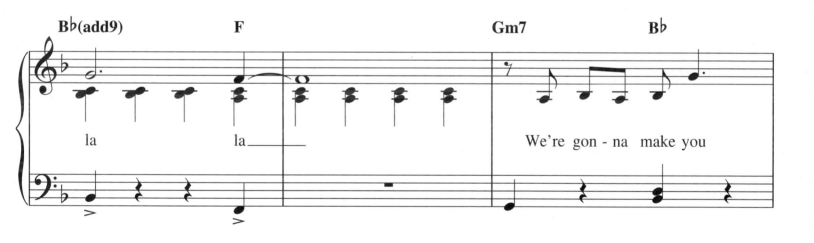

la la We're gon-na make you

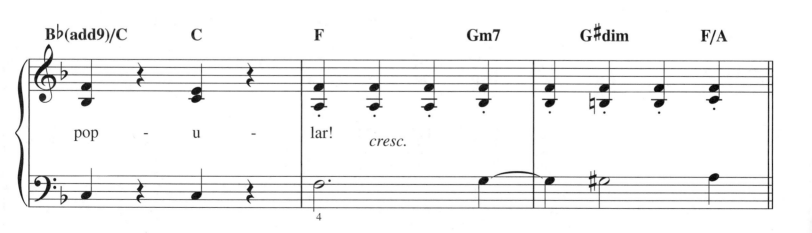

pop-u- lar! *cresc.*

4

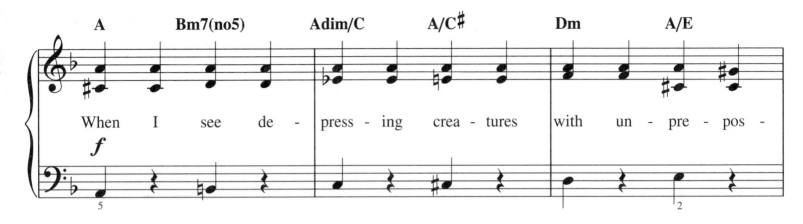

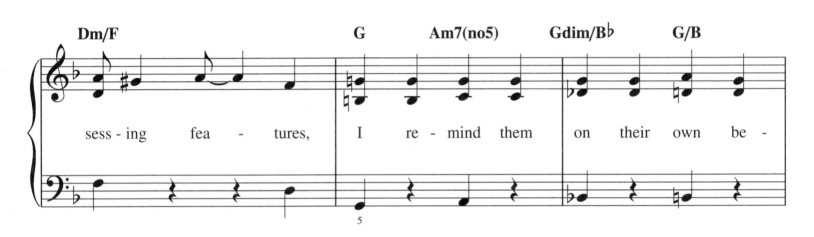

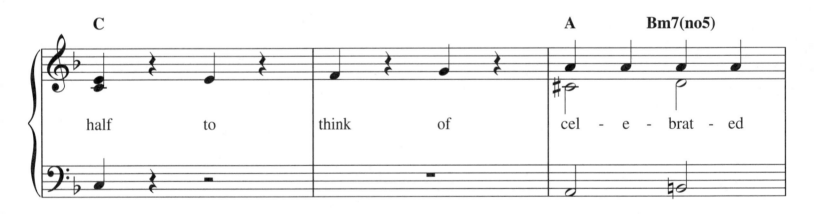

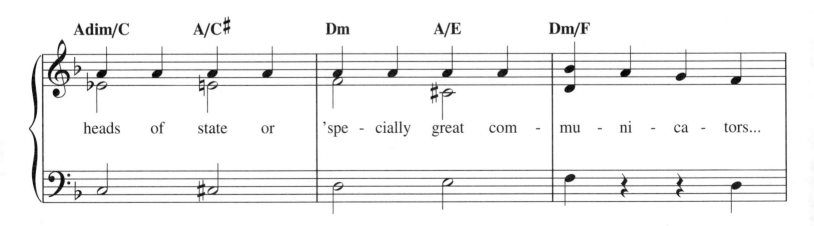

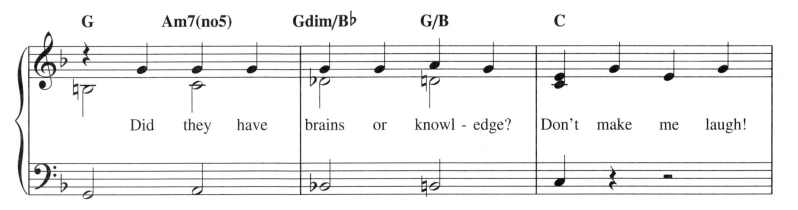

Did they have brains or knowl-edge? Don't make me laugh!

They were pop - u - lar___ *Please!* It's all___ a - bout

pop - u - lar! It's not a - bout ap - ti - tude, it's the

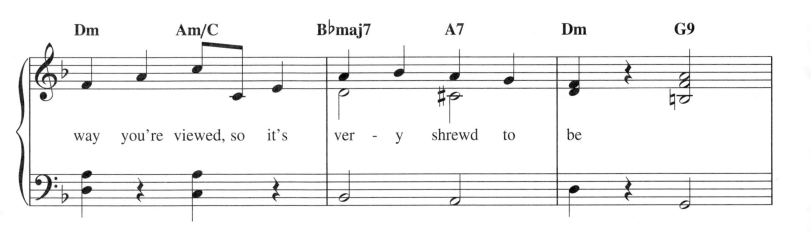

way you're viewed, so it's ver - y shrewd to be

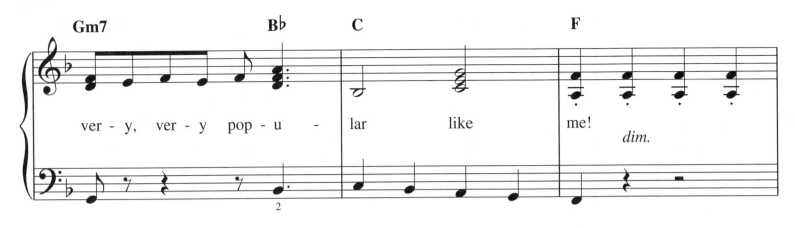

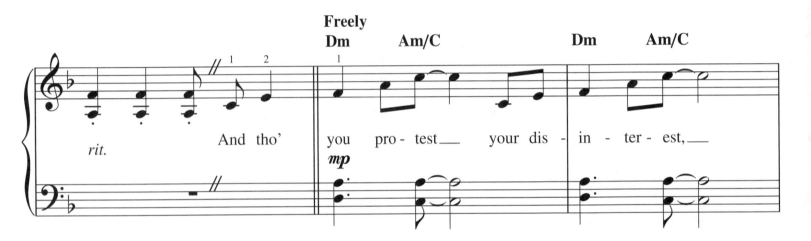

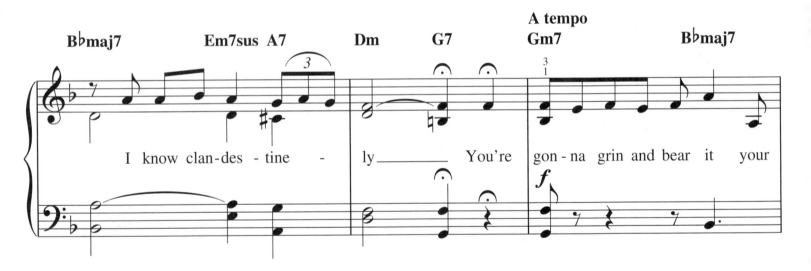

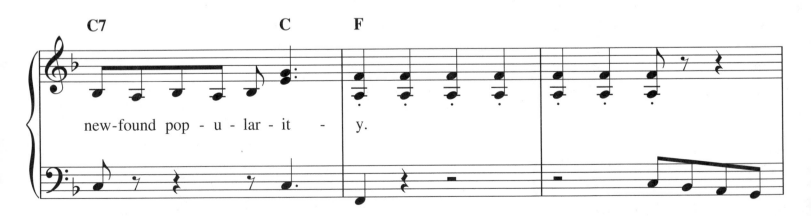

53

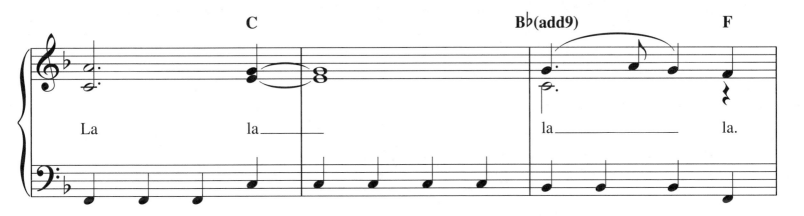

La la   la   la.

You'll be pop - u - lar Just not quite as pop - u -

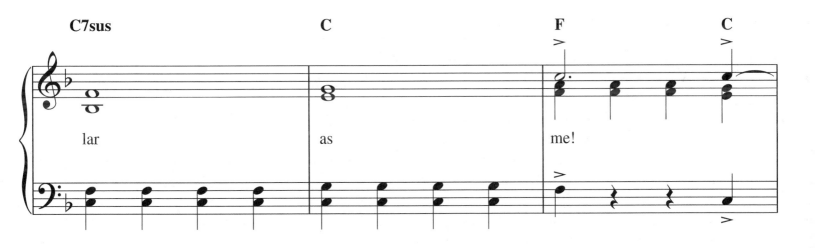

lar   as   me!

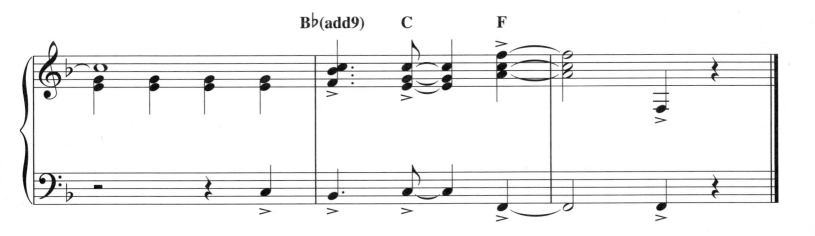

WHAT IS THIS FEELING?

Music and Lyrics by
STEPHEN SCHWARTZ

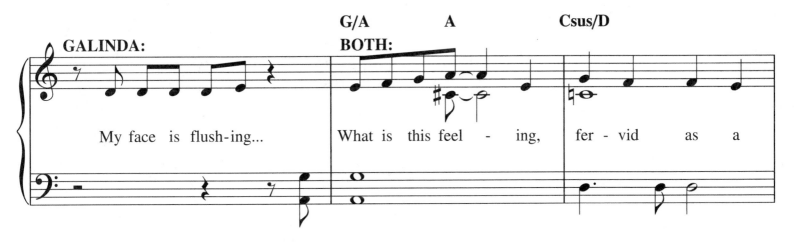

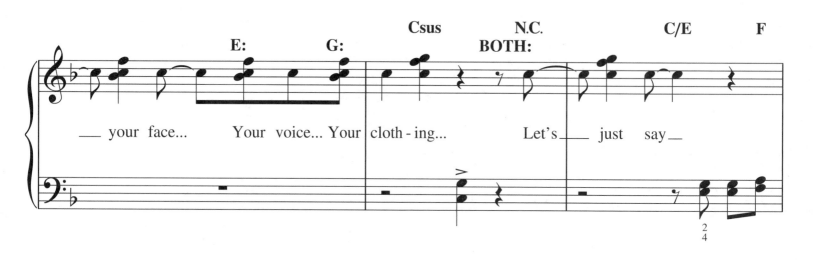

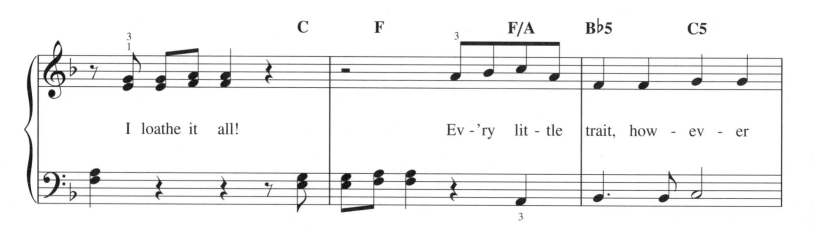

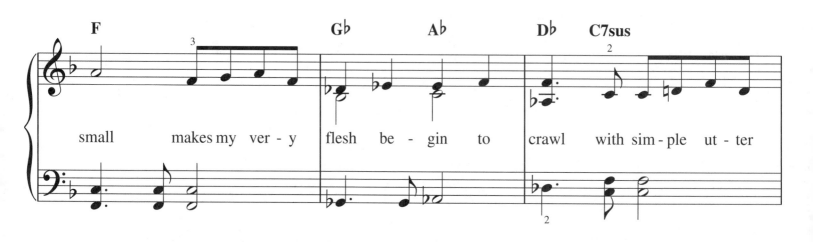

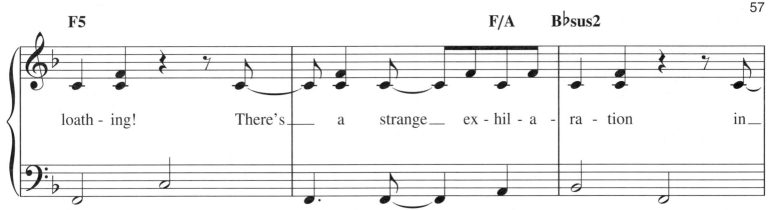

58

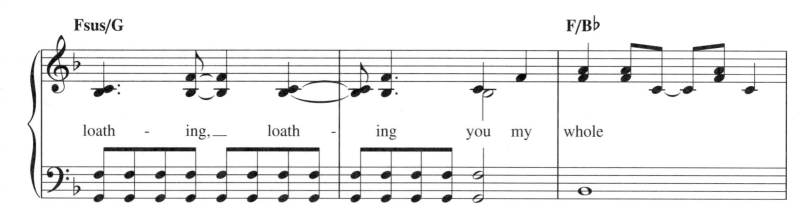

loath - ing, ___ loath - ing you my whole

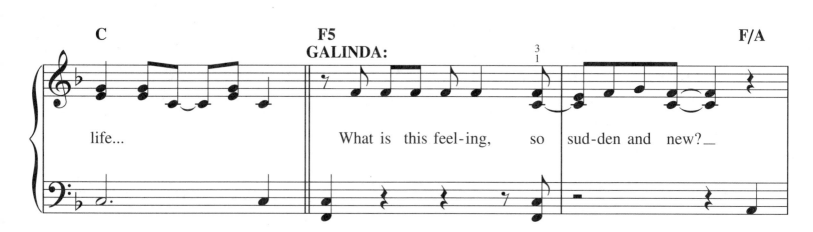

life...

GALINDA:

What is this feel-ing, so sud-den and new? ___

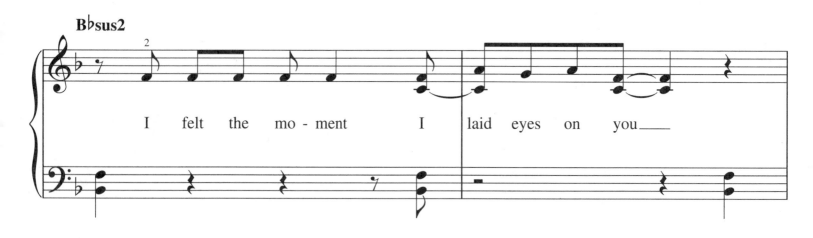

I felt the mo - ment I laid eyes on you ___

My pulse is rush - ing, My head is reel - ing,

ra - tion　　　in＿ such to - tal de - tes - ta - tion

So　pure, so　strong!　　　　Though I　do ad -

mit it came on　fast,＿　　still I do be - lieve that it＿　can

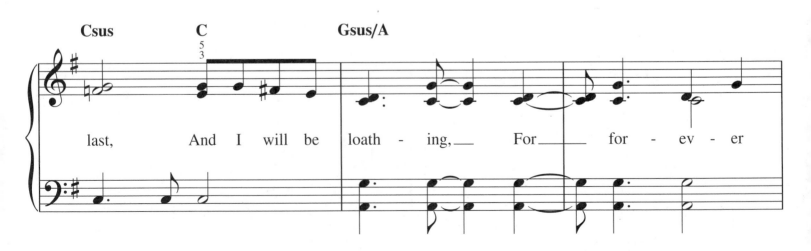

last,　　And I will be　loath - ing,＿ For＿ for - ev - er

loath - ing,_____ Tru - ly, deep - ly

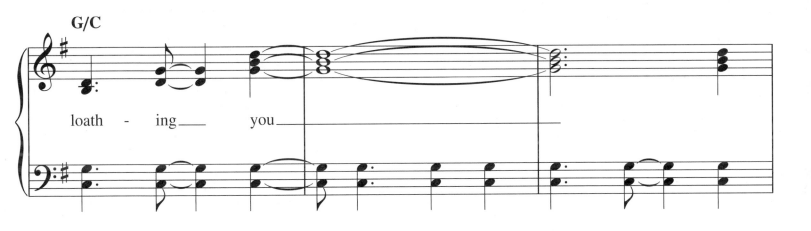

loath - ing____ you____

my whole__ life long!

THE WIZARD AND I

Music and Lyrics by
STEPHEN SCHWARTZ

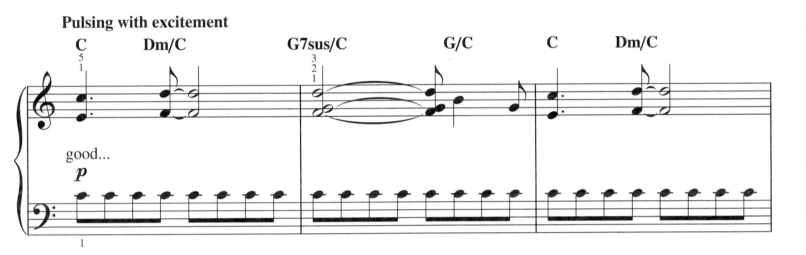

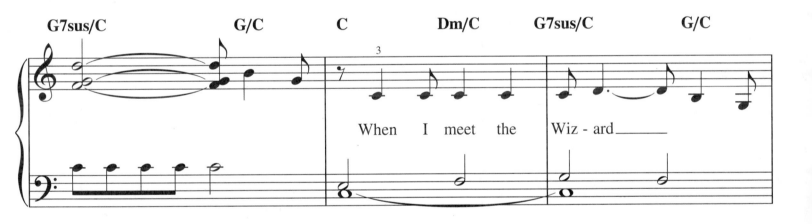

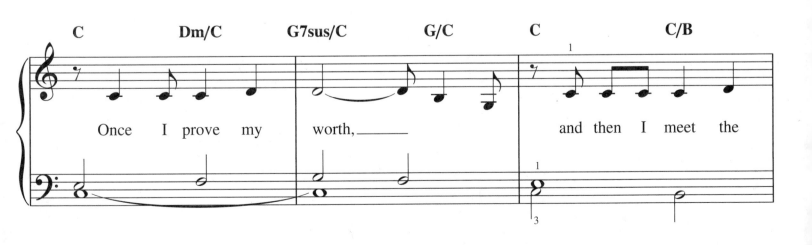

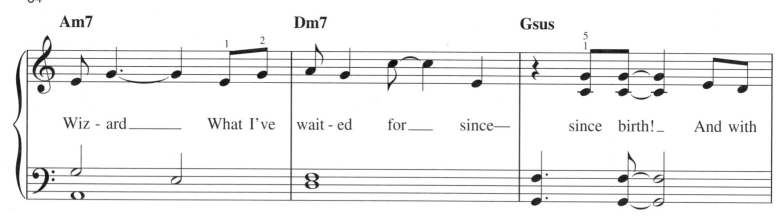

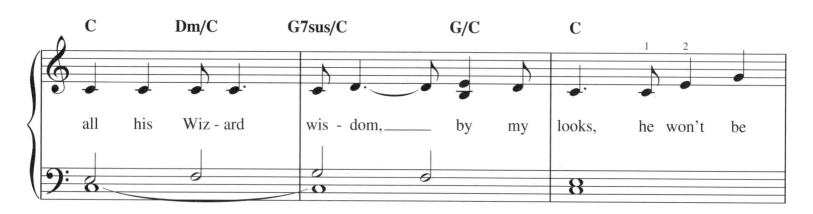

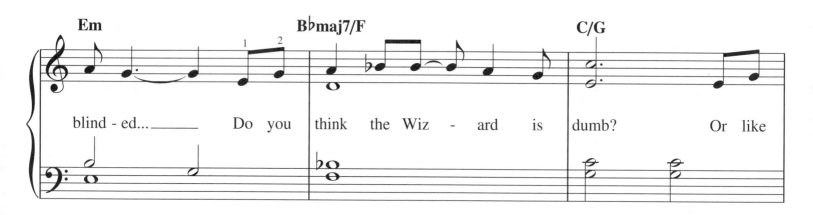

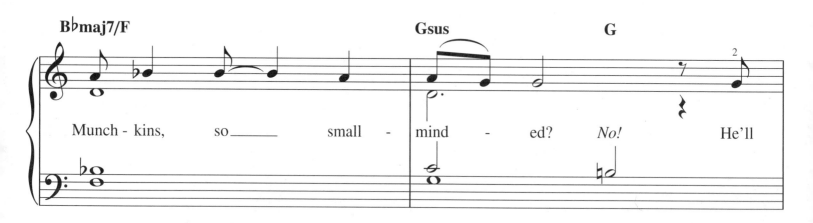

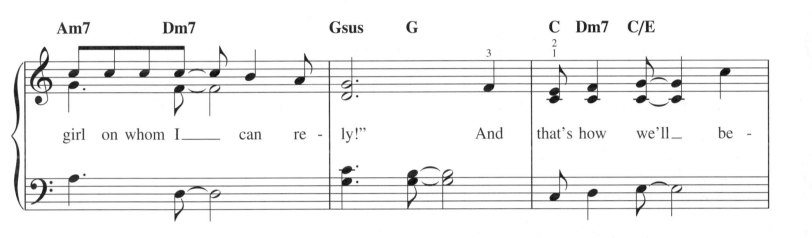

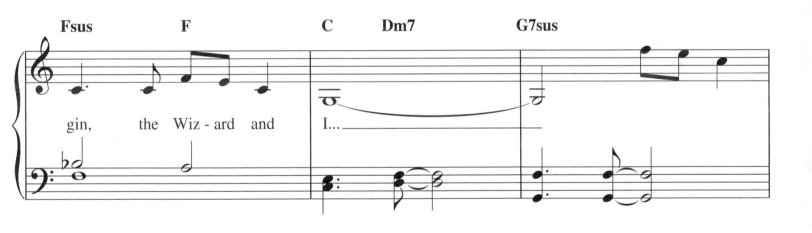

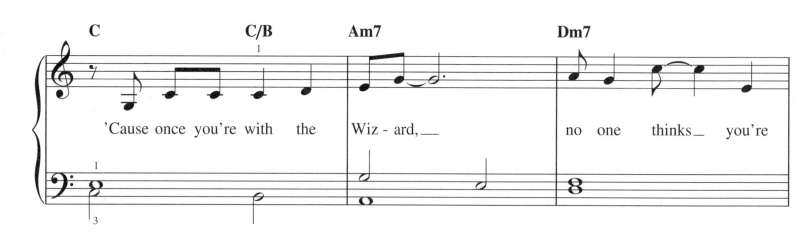

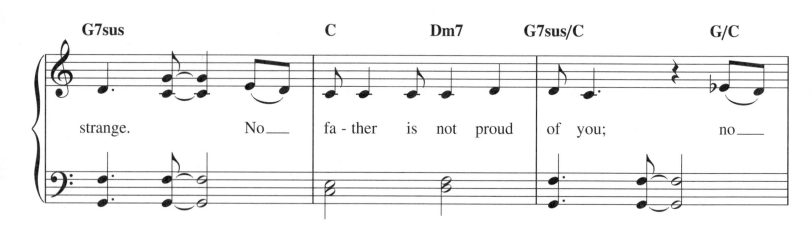

67

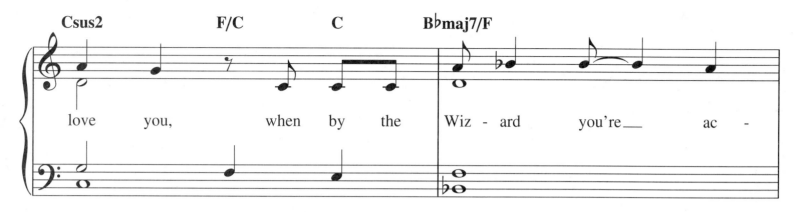

love you, when by the Wiz - ard you're___ ac -

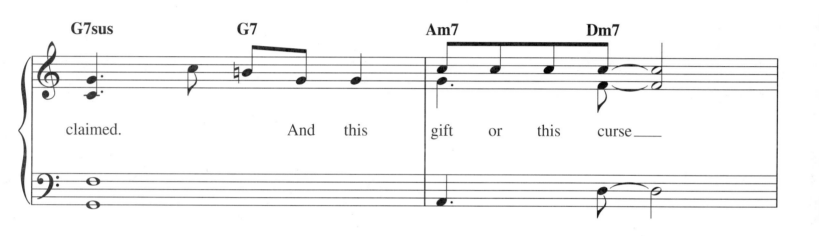

claimed. And this gift or this curse___

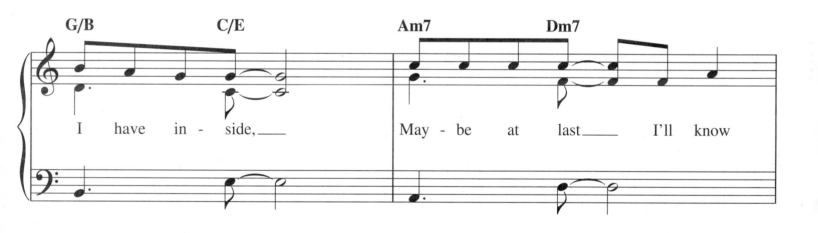

I have in - side,___ May - be at last___ I'll know

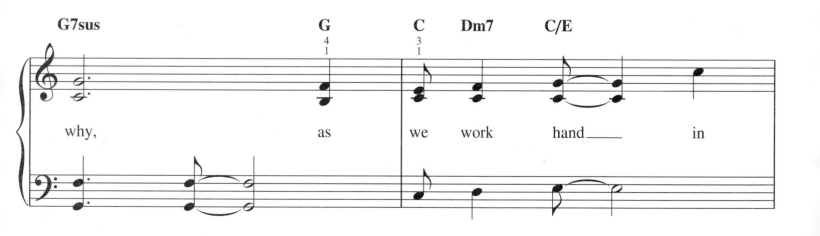

why, as we work hand___ in

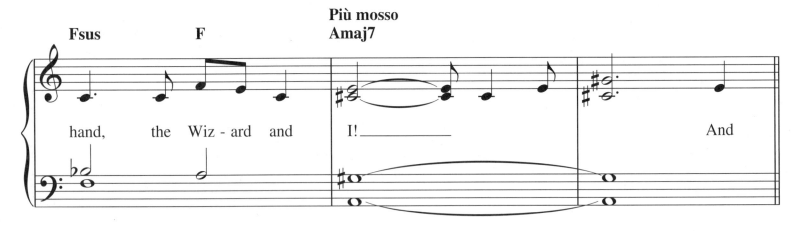

Più mosso

Fsus   F   Amaj7

hand,   the   Wiz - ard   and   I!_____   And

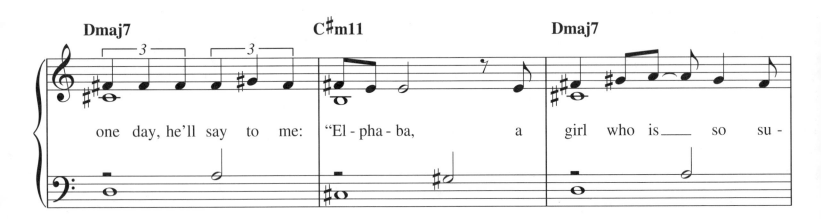

Dmaj7   C#m11   Dmaj7

one   day,   he'll   say   to   me: "El - pha - ba,   a   girl   who   is__   so   su -

C#m11   Fmaj7   Em7(add4)

pe - ri - or—   Should-n't   a   girl__   who's   so   good   in - side__

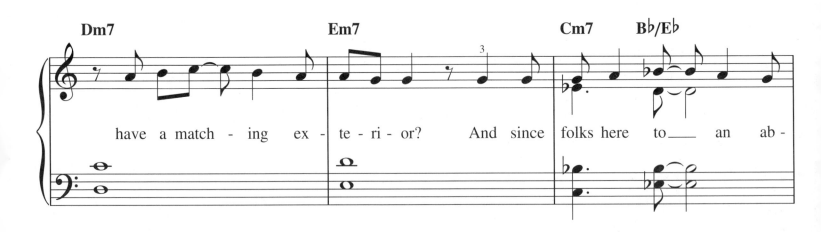

Dm7   Em7   Cm7   Bb/Eb

have   a   match - ing   ex - te - ri - or?   And   since   folks   here   to__   an   ab -

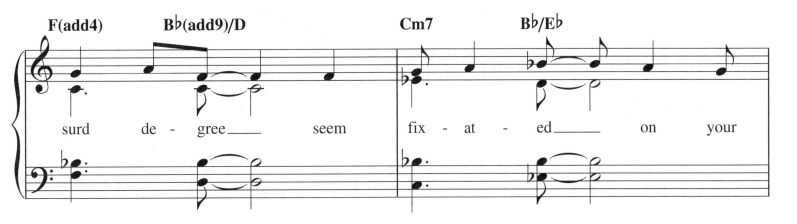

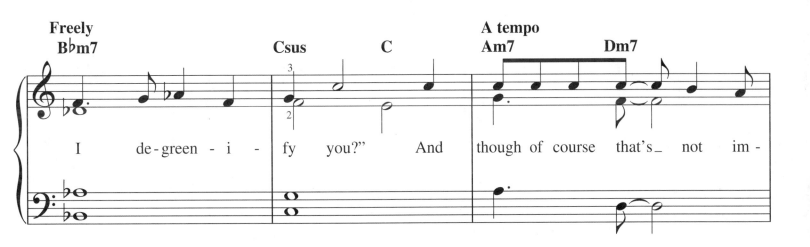

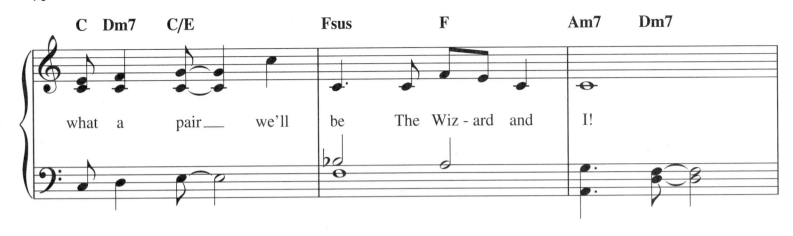

what a pair___ we'll be The Wiz-ard and I!

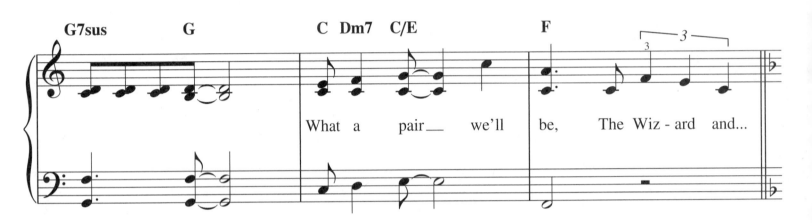

What a pair___ we'll be, The Wiz-ard and...

Dreamily

subito **p**

Un - lim - it - ed,___

___ My fu-ture is___ un - lim - it - ed... And I've just had a

vi-sion al-most like a proph-e-cy— I know, it sounds tru-ly cra-zy, and

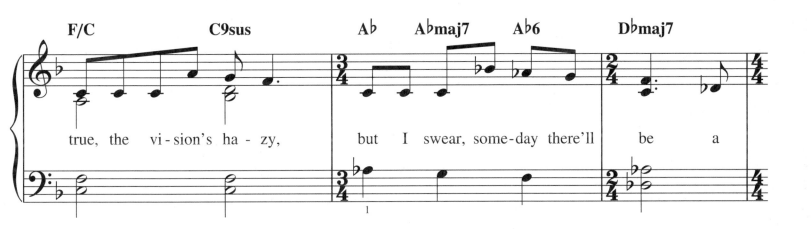

true, the vi-sion's ha-zy, but I swear, some-day there'll be a

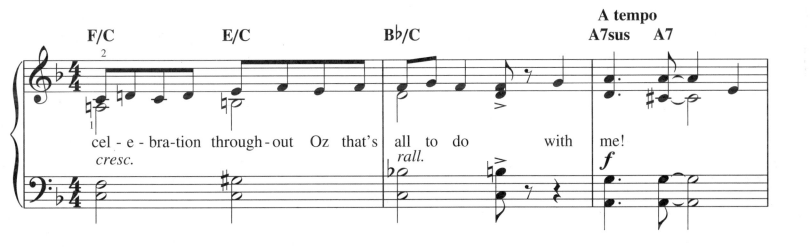

cel-e-bra-tion through-out Oz that's all to do with me!

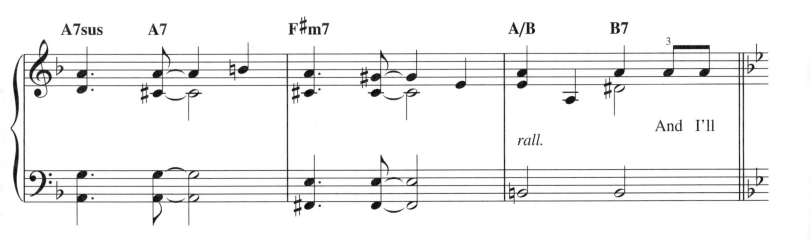

And I'll

Broadly

stand there with the Wiz - ard,_____ feel - ing things I've nev - er

felt, And though I'd nev - er show it, I'll be so
accel.

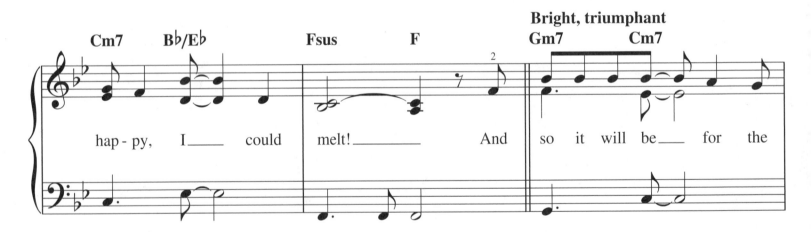

hap - py, I___ could melt!_____ And so it will be___ for the
Bright, triumphant

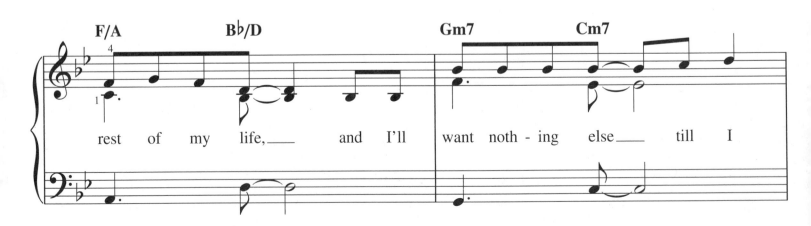

rest of my life,___ and I'll want noth - ing else___ till I

73

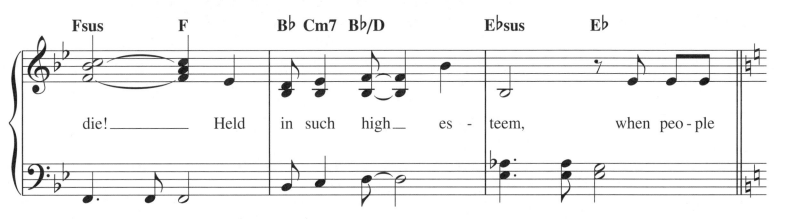

die! _____ Held in such high_ es - teem, when peo - ple

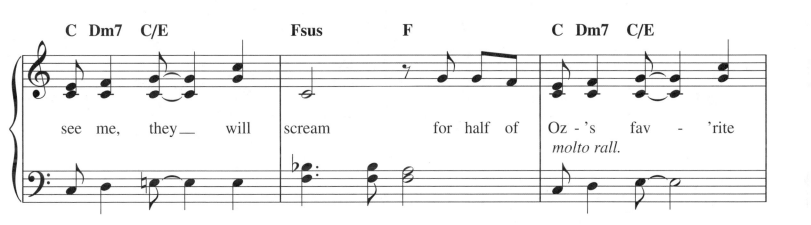

see me, they_ will scream for half of Oz - 's fav - 'rite

team: _____ The Wiz - ard and I!

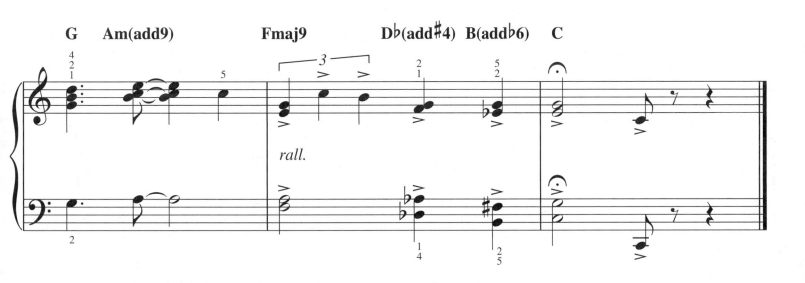

I COULDN'T BE HAPPIER

Music and Lyrics by
STEPHEN SCHWARTZ

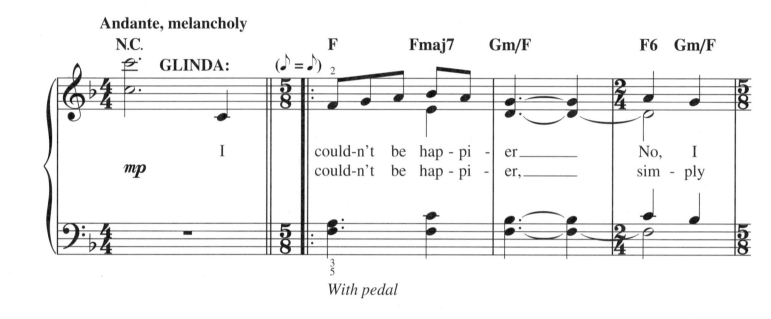

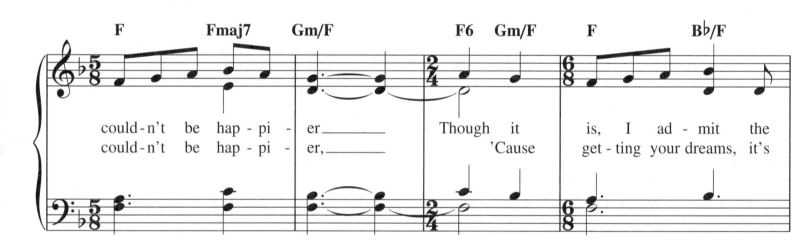

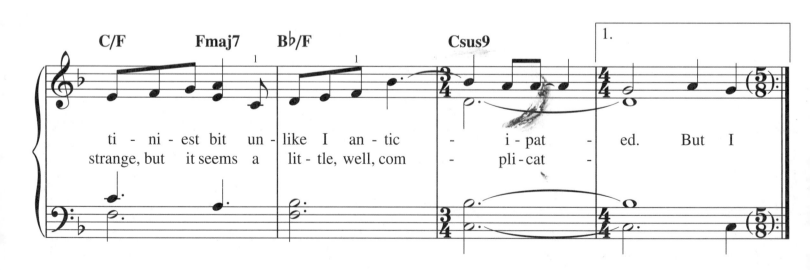

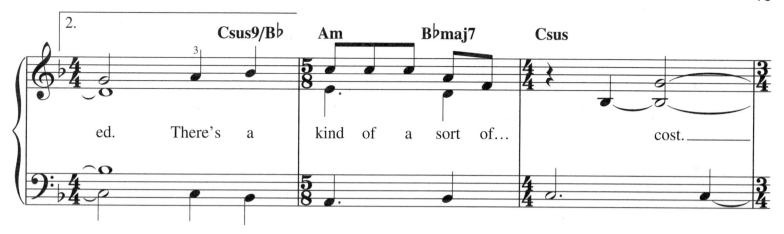

ed. There's a kind of a sort of... cost.____

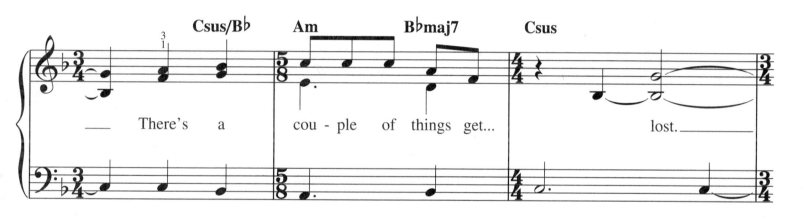

____ There's a cou-ple of things get... lost.____

____ There are bridg-es you cross you did-n't know____ you

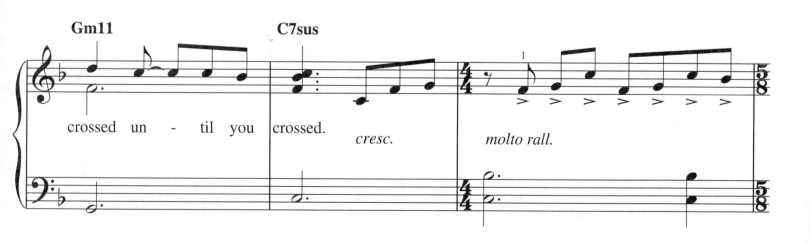

crossed un-til you crossed.

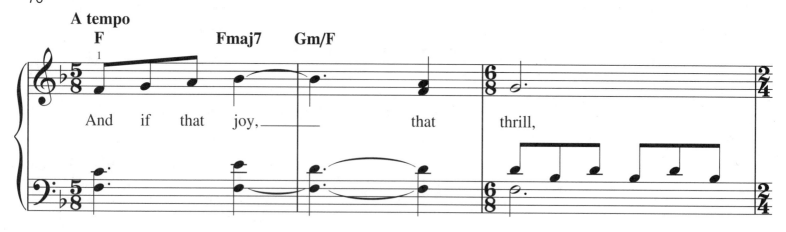

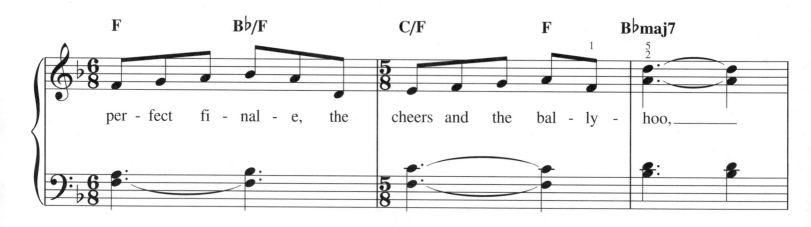

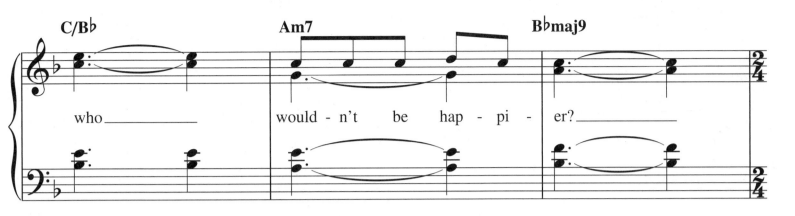

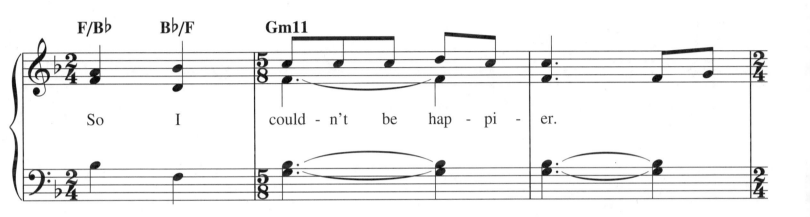

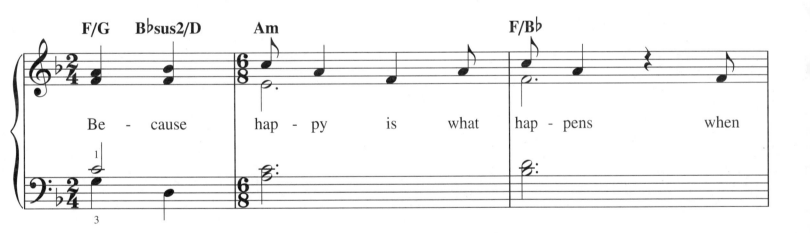

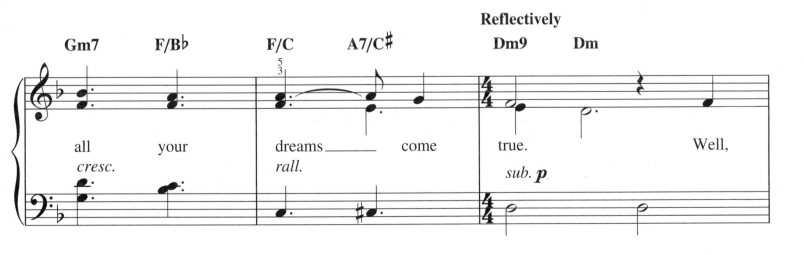

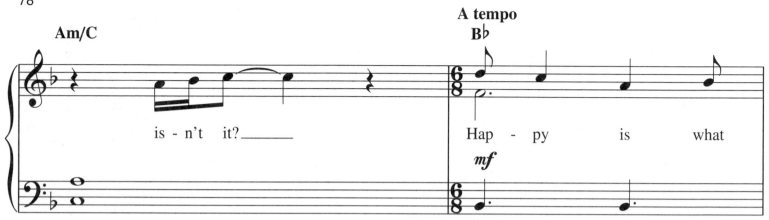

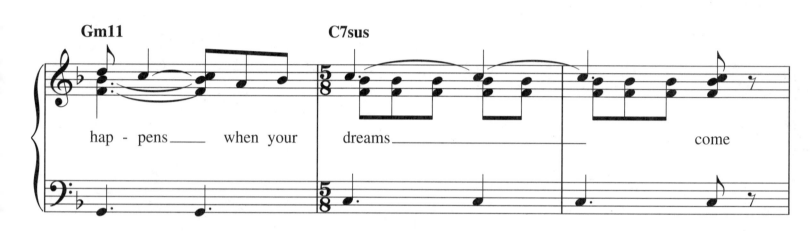

EASY PIANO
CD PLAY-ALONGS
Orchestrated arrangements
with you as the soloist!

This series lets you play along with great accompaniments to songs you know and love! Each book comes with a CD of complete professional performances and includes matching custom arrangements in Easy Piano format. With these books you can: Listen to complete professional performances of each of the songs; Play the Easy Piano arrangements along with the performances; Sing along with the recordings; Play the Easy Piano arrangements as solos, without the CD.

GREAT JAZZ STANDARDS – VOLUME 1
Bewitched • Don't Get Around Much Anymore • How Deep Is the Ocean • It Might As Well Be Spring • My Funny Valentine • Satin Doll • Stardust • and more.
00310916 Easy Piano $14.95

FAVORITE CLASSICAL THEMES – VOLUME 2
Bach: Air on the G String • Beethoven: Symphony No. 5, Excerpt • Gounod: Ave Maria • Grieg: Morning • Handel: Hallelujah Chorus • Pachelbel: Canon • Tchaikovsky: Waltz of the Flowers • and more.
00310921 Easy Piano $14.95

BROADWAY FAVORITES – VOLUME 3
All I Ask of You • Beauty and the Beast • Bring Him Home • Cabaret • Close Every Door • I've Never Been in Love Before • If I Loved You • Memory • My Favorite Things • Some Enchanted Evening.
00310915 Easy Piano $14.95

ADULT CONTEMPORARY HITS – VOLUME 4
Amazed • Angel • Breathe • I Don't Want to Wait • I Hope You Dance • I Will Remember You • I'll Be • It's Your Love • The Power of Love • You'll Be in My Heart.
00310919 Easy Piano $14.95

HIT POP/ROCK BALLADS – VOLUME 5
Don't Let the Sun Go Down on Me • From a Distance • I Can't Make You Love Me • I'll Be There • Imagine • In My Room • Rainy Days and Mondays • Total Eclipse of the Heart • and more.
00310917 Easy Piano $14.95

LOVE SONG FAVORITES – VOLUME 6
Fields of Gold • I Honestly Love You • If • Lady in Red • More Than Words • Save the Best for Last • Three Times a Lady • Up Where We Belong • We've Only Just Begun • You Are So Beautiful.
00310918 Easy Piano $14.95

O HOLY NIGHT – VOLUME 7
Angels We Have Heard on High • God Rest Ye Merry, Gentlemen • It Came upon the Midnight Clear • O Holy Silent Night • What Child Is This? • and more.
00310920 Easy Piano $14.95

A CHRISTIAN WEDDING – VOLUME 8
Cherish the Treasure • Commitment Song • How Beautiful • I Will Be Here • In This Very Room • The Lord's Prayer • Love Will Be Our Home • Parent's Prayer • This Is the Day • The Wedding.
00311104 Easy Piano $14.95

COUNTRY BALLADS – VOLUME 9
Always on My Mind • Could I Have This Dance • Crazy • Crying • Forever and Ever, Amen • He Stopped Loving Her Today • I Can Love You Like That • The Keeper of the Stars • Release Me • When You Say Nothing at All.
00311105 Easy Piano $14.95

MOVIE GREATS – VOLUME 10
And All That Jazz • Chariots of Fire • Come What May • Forrest Gump • I Finally Found Someone • Iris • Mission: Impossible Theme • Tears in Heaven • There You'll Be • A Wink and a Smile.
00311106 Easy Piano $14.95

DISNEY BLOCKBUSTERS – VOLUME 11
Be Our Guest • Can You Feel the Love Tonight • Go the Distance • Look Through My Eyes • Reflection • Two Worlds • Under the Sea • A Whole New World • Written in the Stars • You've Got a Friend in Me.
00311107 Easy Piano $14.95

CHRISTMAS FAVORITES – VOLUME 12
Blue Christmas • Frosty the Snow Man • Here Comes Santa Claus • I'll Be Home for Christmas • Silver Bells • Wonderful Christmastime • and more.
00311257 Easy Piano $14.95

CHILDREN'S SONGS – VOLUME 13
Any Dream Will Do • Do-Re-Mi • It's a Small World • Linus and Lucy • The Rainbow Connection • Splish Splash • This Land Is Your Land • Winnie the Pooh • Yellow Submarine • Zip-A-Dee-Doo-Dah.
00311258 Easy Piano $14.95

CHILDREN'S FAVORITES – VOLUME 14
Alphabet Song • Frere Jacques • Home on the Range • My Bonnie Lies over the Ocean • Oh! Susanna • Old MacDonald • This Old Man • Yankee Doodle • and more.
00311259 Easy Piano $14.95

DISNEY'S BEST – VOLUME 15
Beauty and the Beast • Bibbidi-Bobbidi-Boo • Chim Chim Cher-ee • Colors of the Wind • Friend Like Me • Hakuna Matata • Part of Your World • Someday • When She Loved Me • You'll Be in My Heart.
00311260 Easy Piano $14.95

LENNON & McCARTNEY HITS – VOLUME 16
Eleanor Rigby • Hey Jude • The Long and Winding Road • Love Me Do • Lucy in the Sky with Diamonds • Nowhere Man • Please Please Me • Sgt. Pepper's Lonely Hearts Club Band • Strawberry Fields Forever • Yesterday.
00311262 Easy Piano $14.95

HOLIDAY HITS – VOLUME 17
Christmas Time Is Here • Feliz Navidad • I Saw Mommy Kissing Santa Claus • Jingle-Bell Rock • The Most Wonderful Time of the Year • My Favorite Things • Santa Claus Is Comin' to Town • and more.
00311329 Easy Piano $14.95

HIGH SCHOOL MUSICAL – VOLUME 18
Bop to the Top • Breaking Free • Get'cha Head in the Game • Stick to the Status Quo • We're All in This Together • What I've Been Looking For • When There Was Me and You • and more.
00311752 Easy Piano $14.95

HIGH SCHOOL MUSICAL 2 – VOLUME 19
All for One • Everyday • Fabulous • Gotta Go My Own Way • I Don't Dance • What Time Is It • Work This Out • You Are the Music in Me.
00311753 Easy Piano $14.99

ANDREW LLOYD WEBBER – FAVORITES – VOLUME 20
Another Suitcase in Another Hall • Any Dream Will Do • As If We Never Said Goodbye • I Believe My Heart • Memory • Think of Me • Unexpected Song • Whistle down the Wind • You Must Love Me • and more.
00311775 Easy Piano $14.99

GREAT CLASSICAL MELODIES – VOLUME 21
Arioso • Ave Maria • Fur Elise • Jesu, Joy of Man's Desiring • Lullaby (Cradle Song) • Meditation • Ode to Joy • Romeo and Juliet (Love Theme) • Sicilienne • Theme from Swan Lake • and more.
00311776 Easy Piano $14.99

ANDREW LLOYD WEBBER – HITS – VOLUME 22
Don't Cry for Me Argentina • I Don't Know How to Love Him • Love Changes Everything • The Music of the Night • No Matter What • Wishing You Were Somehow Here Again • With One Look • and more.
00311785 Easy Piano $14.95

Prices, contents and availability subject to change without notice.

FOR MORE INFORMATION, SEE YOUR LOCAL MUSIC DEALER, OR WRITE TO:

HAL•LEONARD®
CORPORATION
7777 W. BLUEMOUND RD. P.O. BOX 13819 MILWAUKEE, WI 53213

www.halleonard.com

0109

It's Easy to Play Your Favorite Songs with Hal Leonard Easy Piano Books

The Best Praise & Worship Songs Ever
The name says it all: over 70 of the best P&W songs today. Titles include: Awesome God • Blessed Be Your Name • Come, Now Is the Time to Worship • Days of Elijah • Here I Am to Worship • Open the Eyes of My Heart • Shout to the Lord • We Fall Down • and more.
00311312 ....$19.95

The Best Songs Ever
Over 70 all-time favorite songs, including: All I Ask of You • Body and Soul • Call Me Irresponsible • Edelweiss • Fly Me to the Moon • The Girl from Ipanema • Here's That Rainy Day • Imagine • Let It Be • Moonlight in Vermont • People • Somewhere Out There • Tears in Heaven • Unforgettable • The Way We Were • and more.
00359223 ....$19.95

Ten Top Hits for Easy Piano
Ten tunes from the top of the charts in 2006: Because of You • Black Horse and the Cherry Tree • Breaking Free • Jesus Take the Wheel • Listen to Your Heart • Over My Head (Cable Car) • The Riddle • Unwritten • Upside Down • You're Beautiful.
00310530 ....$10.95

Jumbo Easy Piano Songbook
200 classical favorites, folk songs and jazz standards. Includes: Amazing Grace • Beale Street Blues • Bridal Chorus • Buffalo Gals • Canon in D • Cielito Lindo • Danny Boy • The Entertainer • Für Elise • Greensleeves • Jamaica Farewell • Marianne • Molly Malone • Ode to Joy • Peg O' My Heart • Rockin' Robin • Yankee Doodle • dozens more!
00311014 ....$19.95

Best Children's Songs Ever
A great collection of over 100 songs, including: Alphabet Song • The Bare Necessities • Beauty and the Beast • Eensy Weensy Spider • The Farmer in the Dell • Hakuna Matata • My Favorite Things • Puff the Magic Dragon • The Rainbow Connection • Take Me Out to the Ball Game • Twinkle, Twinkle Little Star • Winnie the Pooh • and more.
00310360 ....$19.95

150 of the Most Beautiful Songs Ever
Easy arrangements of 150 of the most popular songs of our time. Includes: Bewitched • Fly Me to the Moon • How Deep Is Your Love • My Funny Valentine • Some Enchanted Evening • Tears in Heaven • Till There Was You • Yesterday • You Are So Beautiful • and more. 550 pages of great music!
00311316...$24.95

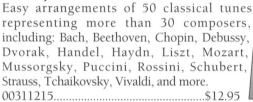

50 Easy Classical Themes
Easy arrangements of 50 classical tunes representing more than 30 composers, including: Bach, Beethoven, Chopin, Debussy, Dvorak, Handel, Haydn, Liszt, Mozart, Mussorgsky, Puccini, Rossini, Schubert, Strauss, Tchaikovsky, Vivaldi, and more.
00311215...$12.95

Today's Country Hits
A collection of 13 contemporary country favorites, including: Bless the Broken Road • Jesus Take the Wheel • Summertime • Tonight I Wanna Cry • When I Get Where I'm Goin' • When the Stars Go Blue • and more.
00290188...$12.95

VH1's 100 Greatest Songs of Rock and Roll
The results from the VH1 show that featured the 100 greatest rock and roll songs of all time are here in this awesome collection! Songs include: Born to Run • Good Vibrations • Hey Jude • Hotel California • Imagine • Light My Fire • Like a Rolling Stone • Respect • and more.
00311110...$27.95

Disney's My First Song Book
16 favorite songs to sing and play. Every page is beautifully illustrated with full-color art from Disney features. Songs include: Beauty and the Beast • Bibbidi-Bobbidi-Boo • Circle of Life • Cruella De Vil • A Dream Is a Wish Your Heart Makes • Hakuna Matata • Under the Sea • Winnie the Pooh • You've Got a Friend in Me • and more.
00310322...$15.95

FOR MORE INFORMATION, SEE YOUR LOCAL MUSIC DEALER,
OR WRITE TO:

HAL•LEONARD®
CORPORATION

7777 W. BLUEMOUND RD. P.O. BOX 13819 MILWAUKEE, WI 53213

Get complete song lists and more at **www.halleonard.com**

Prices, contents, and availability subject to change without notice